Fighting Techniques of a

JAPANESE INFANTRYMAN
1941 – 1945

Other titles in this series:

Fighting Techniques of a

JAPANESE INFANTRYMAN
1941 – 1945

Leo J. Daugherty III

amber
BOOKS

This Amber edition published in 2018
First published in 2002

Published by
Amber Books Ltd
United House
North Road
London N7 NDP
United Kingdom
www.amberbooks.co.uk
Appstore: itunes.com/apps/amberbooksltd
Facebook: www.facebook.com/amberbooks
Twitter: @amberbooks

ISBN: 978-1-78274-600-3

Project Editor: Charles Catton
Editor: Siobhan O'Connor
Design: Graham Curd
Picture Research: Lisa Wren/Tom Walker

Printed in the United Kingdom

Picture credits
Chrysalis Images: 12, 22b, 24, 86. **Mary Evans Picture Library:** 8. **POPPERFOTO:** 36, 39, 68b, 73.
Süddeutscher Verlag: 1, 27, 42, 51b, 52, 54, 56, 57, 58, 59, 60t, 62b, 80, 82. **TRH Pictures:** 6, 10, 15, 16, 17,
18, 20, 21, 22t, 25, 26, 29, 35, 37, 40, 43, 44, 48 (both), 50, 51t, 62-63t, 66, 67, 69, 71, 83, 85, 92t.
TRH/US Army: 31. **TRH/US Marine Corps:** 14, 72-73b, 38, 92b. **TRH/US National Archives:** 9, 12, 30, 32,
34, 46, 78, 79, 88, 90, 91. **TRH/US Navy:** 11. **US Marine Corps.:** 75, 76, 77, 78.

Artwork credits
All illustrations courtesy of Amber Books except the following:
Aerospace Publishing Ltd: 13, 28, 47, 60b, 65, 84.
De AgostiniUK: 33, 45.

CONTENTS

CHAPTER 1

The Martial Tradition of the Japanese Army, 1900–1945

> Before 1945 Japanese society was militaristic; men were raised in a martial manner and called to serve the emperor. The ancient warrior code of *Bushido* still influenced the armed forces in their conduct, and a Japanese soldier was expected to put his loyalty to the emperor above all else.

THE JAPANESE SOLDIER OF WORLD War II was a tough, tenacious and resourceful fighter. From the fields and valleys of Manchuria and China, and the steaming jungles of Burma and the South Pacific, to the coral atolls of the Central Pacific, the Japanese Army demonstrated its fanatical fighting abilities. As American, British, Australian, New Zealand, Soviet and Chinese infantrymen discovered, the Japanese soldier was just as 'good', if not better, as his German counterpart. More important, however, was the Japanese soldier's application of modern technology to battlefield situations. While the Japanese Army remained primarily an infantry-based force, the Japanese soldier had at his disposal a vast arsenal of weapons, including tanks, small arms, aircraft and artillery. When this was combined with the tactical and operational doctrines of offensive and defensive warfare, the 'warriors' of the Imperial Japanese Empire proved to be more than a match for their Western counterparts.

The origins of the Japanese infantryman's fighting abilities lie in Japan's warrior past. Schooled in the 'spirit' and ways of the samurai warrior, the Japanese soldier, both officer and enlisted man, was a skilled individual fighter indoctrinated from an early age in the art of warfare. In fact, the strong military presence marking Japan's internal history from the twelfth century AD through to its initial contacts with the West in 1856 was to influence greatly the course of Japanese history, and it would also have a great influence on its development as a modern nation. Not only were the samurai felt to be the masters of the political fate of the nation, but they were also considered the leaders of the popular conscience. The morale and spirit of the warrior was as important to their influence on society as was their material power.

Indeed, recognition of this last fact witnessed the growth of a military or para-government administered by the office of the *shogun*, or generalissimo. Unlike in Europe during the Middle Ages, the samurai superseded the aristocracy in both cultural and political leadership. In time, Japanese society became militarised, based on the feudal notions of service and loyalty to the nation. Along with Japan's contacts with Confucian China, the development of a Neo-Confucianist philosophy in turn led to the development of the code of the warrior, or *Bushido*. It was the 'spirit of the warrior', or *Bushido*, that drove Japan to first open its doors to the West in 1856 with the arrival of the American Commodore Matthew C. Perry, USN, and later facilitated its steady territorial growth in north-east Asia. Commencing in 1895, with Japan's acquisition of Taiwan, through to the end of World War I in 1918, when her armies dominated the German concessions in China, Japan began expanding her empire. During the interwar era (1919–1941), she stood

Left: Victorious Japanese troops shout 'Banzai' upon hearing the news of another victory in early 1942. In the early months of the war, like their German allies, the Japanese swept all opposition before them.

Above: Three samurai warriors in their ornate, traditional fighting dress, pictured in the early years of the twentieth century.
The influence of the historical samurai class contributed to the increasing militarism of the Japanese people prior to World War II.

second only to the United States in terms of political and military influence in Asia.

What facilitated Japan's growth during this period was the steady development of its armed forces, most notably the growth of its Army and Navy along Western lines imbued with the spirit and code of the warrior. It was this spirit that propelled Japan's armed forces across the Pacific and ultimately led to her defeat in September 1945 at the hands of the same Western Allies that had originally introduced the concepts of modern warfare to Japan's warrior caste.

Much like its Western contemporaries, the Japanese Army of World War II had been conditioned for war during the first three decades of the twentieth century.

While the Japanese Army learned its fighting techniques – insofar as modern warfare was concerned – from the experiences of Western armies before and during World War I (1914–1918), many of its warfighting and training techniques had become ingrained long before the arrival of the French, German and, to a lesser degree, British training missions in Japan after the Restoration in 1868.

From the twelfth century until 1945, the samurai class superseded the old aristocracy in both its political and cultural leadership. Over the centuries, Thomas Clearly argues, 'certain aspects of Zen and Neo-Confucianism were espoused by the samurai', which led to the development of *Bushido* (the code of the warrior). With Zen's advocacy of rigid discipline or a civil form of militarism (at times hidden or obscured under the cover of Zen or Zen martial arts) and Confucianism's paternalistic emphasis, Japanese society became susceptible to the militarism of the samurai class. This quickly united feudal Japan's internal disunity, in the same way that Bismarck, helped by the Prussian Army, unified Germany from 1864 onwards. There is, in fact, as Clearly states, an 'indelible trace of militaristic influence on Japanese Zen as well as Zen influence on the Japanese military', and it became difficult to separate Zen and Confucianism when it came to understanding the Japanese martial tradition; both philosophies affected the political and cultural life of the nation. In fact, Clearly argues that Zen Buddhism, as preached by the Zen Monk Nantembo (1839–1925), had a more direct impact on Japanese militarism than the state religion, Shinto, as many prominent civilians and military men became attracted to Nantembo's preachings during the early twentieth century.

Adding to the impact of Zen and Confucianism on Japanese martial arts were the impact of both Taoism and the Shinto religion. After nearly a century of civil war, Japan had been reunified through the impact of the samurai class on Japanese society. The famous swordsman Miyamoto Musashi contrasted the impact of Zen and Confucianism on Japanese culture in his *Book of the Five Spheres*. He wrote: 'Buddhism is a way of helping people. Confucianism is a way of civilization.' As Japanese militarism developed in the late nineteenth century, both traditions became intertwined with the development of the samurai, which in time became a complete socio-cultural lifestyle, hence the origins of modern Japanese militarism.

JAPANESE MILITARISM AND *BUSHIDO*

Musashi's writings serve as the key to understanding the Japanese art of warfare as it developed in the late nineteenth and twentieth centuries. Musashi wrote that 'the art of war was among the various traditional Ways of Japanese culture, to be studied and practiced by political leaders as well as by professional warriors'. He wrote in *Five Spheres*: 'the arts of warfare are the science of military experts. Leaders in particular practice these arts, and soldiers should also know this science. In the present day there are no warriors with accurate understanding of the science of martial arts.' In fact, Musashi placed particular emphasis on martial arts, writing: 'individual warriors should strengthen their own martial arts as much as practical under the circumstances … In China and

Japan, practitioners of this science have been legendary as masters of martial arts. Warriors should not fail to learn this science.' The emphasis Musashi placed on martial arts and culture stems from the classical Chinese philosophical concepts of warriorhood and its balanced combination of practical learning in both cultural and martial arts. In fact, as emphasised in both the classical Chinese and Japanese traditions, the training of the warrior was 'considered to be one of the most important tasks of culture'. In both countries, warriors were taught cultural arts, while scholars were schooled in martial arts. This practice was later taken up by the upper-class samurai warriors in Japan where, as Clearly states, 'the identification of the civil and military élites was more complete and longer lasting than in China'.

In order to maintain this identification with both Zen and Confucian principles, Japanese soldiers were taught to value such personal qualities as allegiance to the Emperor; self-sacrifice and deprivation; faith; trust in both officers and fellow soldiers; and uprightness, thriftiness, valour, frugality, honour and a highly developed sense of shame. This in turn led the samurai (and the Japanese soldier) to accept the eighth-century practice of *seppuku* or *hara-kiri* (ritual suicide) by stabbing their stomach and an assistant cutting off their head. This is in itself important, in that it has been the subject of much myth in attempting to

Below: Divine leader of a people already conditioned for war: Emperor Hirohito, mounted on his horse Shira-Yuki, inspects Japanese troops at the Yoyo parade ground before their departure for China in 1940.

understand the Japanese soldier and the factors that motivated him on the battlefield. Most important is the simple fact that death and the possibility of death was a constant feature of everyday Japanese life in the feudal era. Musashi reiterated this view when he wrote:

'People usually assume that all warriors think about is getting used to the imminent possibility of death. As far as the process of death is concerned, warriors are not the only ones who die. All classes of people know their duty, are ashamed to neglect it and realize that death is inevitable. There is no difference among social groups in this respect.'

Musashi, in fact, dismissed the notion that all a warrior thought about was this awareness of imminent death. Instead, he linked the idea of imminent death with that of the Buddhist concept of near death in order to explain the warrior's 'acceptance' of his fate in battle. Musashi went one step further in his advocacy of the warrior's overriding need to win. He wrote in *Five Spheres* that 'the way of carrying out the martial arts of warriors is in all events based on excelling others. Whether in winning an

individual duel, or winning a fight with several people, one thinks of serving the interests of one's employer, of serving one's own interests, of becoming well known and socially established. This is all possible by martial arts.'

This identification can be seen in the fact that *Bushido*, the code of the warrior, incorporated the same principles advocated by Musashi in his *Five Spheres*, including the concepts of heroism, death and honour. Despite the fact that the samurai class and the feudal order in which it flourished had been abolished in the last half of the nineteenth century by the Emperor Meiji, through the royal decree known as the Imperial Rescript issued in 1873, the Japanese nonetheless retained the code of *Bushido*. While the royal decree did bring an end to Japan's feudal era, it also served as the basis for the modern Japanese Army. The

Below: Funeral rites for a Japanese soldier killed in China. The remains are to be entombed in the Japanese war memorial honouring all slain soldiers. The code of *Bushido* emphasised the importance of loyalty and duty over self-preservation.

Imperial Rescript contained 'Five Words' which served as a code of conduct for both the officer and the enlisted man. It decreed that:

1. A soldier must do his duty for his country.
2. A soldier must be courteous.
3. A soldier must show courage in war.
4. A soldier must keep his word.
5. A soldier must live simply.

As for the importance of this code of conduct, both the Japanese officer and the enlisted man took these five edicts seriously. In fact, in time it became embodied in the *Senjinkun*, or soldier's code, used by Japanese troops during World War II. As one former Japanese officer wrote after that conflict: 'We worked hard at our training, keeping the "Five Words" in our hearts. I think they are principles we should all live by.' Japanese Prime Minister General Hideki Tojo constantly reminded his troops of their obligation to fight either to extinction or to 'kill themselves' in the course of their duties, as embodied in the soldier's code.

Broken down further, the *Senjinkun* is explicit in its message: devotion to duty and the Emperor. As for loyalty, the code reminded the Japanese soldier of the need for loyalty, which was considered 'his essential duty'. The *Senjinkun* stated: 'Remember that the protection of the state and the maintenance of its power depend upon the strength of its arms … Bear in mind that duty is weightier than a mountain, while death is lighter than a feather …' Japanese soldiers were likewise expected to be courteous to each other and to a defeated enemy. While this may seem surprising given the combat record of Japanese forces in China and the Pacific, the code of *Bushido* is explicit in its condemnation of soldiers who fail to show compassion to

Above: An example of the Japanese willingness to embrace death in the course of duty: a 'Zeke' aircraft in a suicidal attack. The photograph was taken on board the USS *White Plains* during the battle for Leyte Gulf in the Philippines in October 1944.

civilians and enemies alike. Insofar as respect for authority is concerned, the *Senjinkun* specified that soldiers must render total obedience to orders from superiors. In short, 'inferiors should regard the orders from their superiors as issuing directly from the Emperor'.

Importance of Valour

The warrior code specified that a soldier must display valour. Here, the Japanese soldier was to respect an 'inferior' enemy and to fear his superiors', all the while carrying out one's duty as a soldier or a sailor, in other words, as the *Senjinkun* stated, 'true valour'. Soldiers were expected to value faithfulness and righteousness. Faithfulness implied that a Japanese soldier must always keep his word. At the same time, Japanese officers constantly reminded soldiers of the righteousness in his cause and the need to carry out all of his duties. Finally, the soldier's code specified that a soldier must live simply at all times, avoiding 'luxury, effeminate behaviour and extravagance'.

In of all these, the *Senjinkun* outlined that, above all else, a soldier' s duty was to fight and, if necessary, die for the Emperor. While some Japanese soldiers refused to go so far as to kill themselves as World War II came to an end, many were more than willing either to kill themselves when surrounded or to fight to 'extinction', as was the case on Peleliu and Saipan (1944) and on Iwo Jima (1945). Part of this fanaticism or fatalistic resignation was ingrained in the young Japanese Army recruits (both officer and enlisted) during an intensive three months of indoctrination which 'changed them into fanatics, ready to die for their emperor, their country and the honour of their regiments'.

This fanaticism likewise found its way into the concept of blind obedience to orders and superiors. Saburo Sakai, who served in the Japanese Navy during World War II, recalled that this fanaticism, inculcated by their petty officers and noncommissioned officers (NCOs), had 'within six months made human cattle of every one of us. We never dared to question orders, to doubt authority, to do anything but immediately carry out all the commands of our superiors. We were automatons who obeyed without thinking.'

Yet this does not totally explain why Japanese soldiers, sailors and airmen were willing to accept death so readily. A better explanation comes from the fact that the Malayan ancestors of the modern Japanese had both dash and bravery, coupled with the traits of obedience and loyalty they had acquired from the Mongols. These qualities already existed in the average Japanese soldier and thus only needed proper cultivation and exploitation to be

Above: An honour guard greets Japanese premier Hideki Tojo on an inspection visit to Manila in May 1943. To the left of the saluting premier can be seen General Waji, Director General of the Japanese Government of Occupation in the Philippines.

Below: A sombre Sapporo crowd pays its respects to victims of the war in the northern Pacific – an increasingly common sight as the war drew on. The soldiers carry the remains of dead Japanese soldiers killed fighting US forces on Attsu in the Aleutian islands.

brought to the fore. Developed through intensive training, the Japanese soldier proved that he could fight bravely and with an enormous amount of dash and élan, while still accepting orders from his superiors and obeying them without question.

RELIGION AND *BUSHIDO*

Part of this ability to fight to one's death while blindly accepting orders was the incorporation of *Bushido* with the state religion of Shinto in 1867. Twice a year, celebrations are held at the *Yasakuni* or Army Shrine in Tokyo, where the names of fallen soldiers are placed in an ark and carried to an altar. Here, Shinto priests carried out an elaborate ceremony that deified them. This gave rise to the accepted belief that if a soldier were to die in battle, he would achieve lasting immortality and live in concert with the gods. This deification of the war dead and military service itself also took place within the framework of the official version of State Shinto during the Meiji Restoration in 1868. This was due to its legal and ceremonial relationship with the life and the institutions of the nation as a whole.

The state version of the Shinto religion likewise came to embody the principle of *Hakko Ichi-u* ('the whole world under one roof') and thus served to justify Japan's policy of expansion during the 1930s and 1940s. Part of the concept of *Hakko Ichi-u* was based on the beliefs of the legendary first emperor of Japan, Jimmu Tenno, who advanced the messianic idea that the 'Japanese people [be] taught that their state has developed out of the distant past under the formative influence of a divine commission to expand sovereignty and righteousness over ever widening territories'. In short, expansion became a 'heavenly task' under the precepts of Jimmu Tenno. This in fact became the rallying cry that Japan's leaders used to mobilise the 'national spirit' and inspire loyalty with an idealism commensurate with the sacrifices demanded of it. In fact, Admiral Mitsumasa Yonai stated prior to the launching of Japan's expansion into South-east Asia in 1940 that 'the principle of the whole world under one roof embodies the spirit in which the Empire was founded by Jimmu Tenno'. Both Prince Konoye and an unnamed war minister claimed that the basic aim of Japanese national policy was in the unification of all the world into a happy society and the firm establishment of world peace in accordance with the lofty spirit of *Hakko Ichi-u*. This goal could only be achieved through the use of military power, which in turn elevated the military might of Japan into a 'divine soldiery that is sent to bring life to all things'.

Divine Mission

Furthermore, this so-called divine mission meant that all aspects of the Japanese state were to be subordinated to that of achieving *Hakko Ichi-u* through the use of military force. According to this, the 'principal agency for the fulfilment of Japan's mission of benevolent destiny [was] her army' Thus, the 'army [was] established on the unique and impregnable foundation of sole and immediate responsibility to the sacred throne. In such manner there is imparted to the military command the quality of inviolability that attaches to the divine emperor himself.' Thus, it could be said without any hesitation that the entire educational process that a Japanese student underwent while attending school, as well as as an Army recruit, was set up in order to secure and reinforce this idea of absolute obedience on the part of the subjects of the state. Based on the idea of *Hakko Ichi-u*

and State Shinto, D.C. Holtom argues that 'whatever a Japanese soldier did, he did so in the name of the Emperor. In turn, whatever a Japanese soldier did during World War II, particularly in the extension of the power and glory of Japan throughout the world, and in the obedience to the commands of his superior officers, has behind it the authority of an absolute divine initiative. It possesses the quality of religious finality; it is coming from God.'

Japanese military leaders in turn incorporated parts of the *Hakko Ichi-u* into a religious finality of obedience, state service, bravery and loyalty, and then passed these on to the young officers and enlisted men through the *Senjinkun*, or soldier's code. Japanese military leaders placed heavy emphasis on what they called the soldierly spirit, embodied in the *Senjinkun*, whereby great attention was paid to the training of both officers and men to observe the seven 'military virtues' of loyalty, valour, patriotism, obedience, humility, morality and honour. Special lectures on such diverse subjects as ancient warriors, national heroes and national

civil and military figures were given to the men in order to inculcate these virtues. This was all part of a soldier's spiritual training, or *seishin kyoiku*, which occupied an important part of a Japanese soldier's training. Other methods utilised to ingrain loyalty and bravery in the recruits included field trips to battlefields and museums, and visits by royal and other officials. Officers and NCOs also served to personify these values among the new officers and enlisted recruits. Japanese Army training officers and NCOs gave talks and lectures on the necessity of serving the Army faithfully. They likewise nailed various texts and sayings on the walls of mess halls and barracks with patriot slogans and poetry in order to remind

Right: Although this Japanese captain is a tank officer, he carries a traditional sword as well as a Type 94 pistol, a poor design that frequently jammed or fired without warning. He wears the leather helmet and goggles issued to Japanese tank crews.

the soldiers of their responsibility to remain loyal to the Emperor. One last method used by Japanese military officials to instil patriotism among boys approaching military age was to stage re-enactments of famous battles in villages and towns throughout Japan.

Taking this one step further, failure on the battlefield, much as Musashi wrote, was seen as akin to failing faithfully to serve the Emperor and hence the nation as a whole. In fact, it was failure to win – an important element of Japanese society then and now – that caused Japanese officers and enlisted men to commit ritual suicide, rather than surrender. Failure to win on the battlefield (or elsewhere) in time became equated with disloyalty, and suicide became a means of rectifying defeat on the battlefield. Since Shintoism was embodied as a national cult, with the Emperor as its temporal as well as spiritual head, it was thus natural that the Seven Military Virtues – as well as the *Senjinkun* – became an integral part of the soldier's sole reason for existence. In fact, this factor alone guaranteed that the Army portrayed itself as the chief mediating agency between the Emperor and the people. This idea was constantly reinforced, as even the service rifles bore the imprint of the Emperor and served to remind the ordinary soldier of his duty to the Mikado. The Japanese soldier considered service to the Emperor as a means of worshipping god, and so sacrifice of one's service

and, if necessary, life on the battlefield became synonymous with service to the state.

MILITARY EFFICIENCY AND *BUSHIDO*

This devotion to duty and desire for sacrifice was further transferred to the preparation, training and maintenance of military efficiency. Here, the Japanese military soldier employed what is called the *kiai*, a mysterious force or source of power within each man which can be reached by his own effort. This was the basis for the Japanese martial arts and military efficiency. *Ki*, which refers to the 'mind or will', and *ai*, a contraction of the Japanese verb *awasu* – meaning 'to unite' – came to be a motivational power associated with the desire to overcome an opponent. Hence the principle of mind over matter, which is at the heart of the Japanese sports of judo and karate.

The impact of *kiai* on the samurai was enormous. Soon, samurai warriors (and hence Japanese soldiers) came to believe that there was no limit to the powers of human

Below: Three US marines stand ready as a lone Japanese soldier, having tried to blow himself up along with the American soldiers, is forced to surrender on Namur in the Marshall Islands in February 1944. Japanese prisoners were rare until late in the war.

Above: Not all Japanese soldiers committed *hara-kiri* like the two officers pictured here on the island of Okinawa in 1945. Of the 120,000 Japanese defenders of Okinawa, more than 90 per cent were killed in action.

there then developed the notion that a samurai – of any ranks – should never refuse an order because it was impossible to carry out. The word 'impossible' thus did not exist in the Japanese Army.

Japanese soldiers were taught to attack, even if outnumbered or lacking in equipment or proper support. There were numerous incidents during World War II where Japanese troops launched attacks without artillery, air or other forms of support against fortified positions manned by machine guns and other supporting arms. As occurred on Guadalcanal in August 1942 and throughout the Pacific War, Japanese soldiers needlessly threw themselves against US, British and Australian positions, resulting in many of them being killed without even coming close to achieving their objectives. Japanese commanders never refused such an order despite the odds stacked against success. A Japanese officer's or soldier's refusal to attack constituted a grave violation of *Bushido*.

Bushido is solely concerned with relations between the samurai and their conduct in battle. While *Bushido* has

endurance. Japanese military officials cultivated the spirit of *kiai* into a motivational rationale for the military's emphasis on hard training. The belief existed that there was no conceivable limit to what a Japanese recruit was capable of doing if properly motivated. If successfully cultivated, the spirit of *kiai* or *hara* ('guts') was thought to make a soldier who was capable of superhuman efforts. This in turn resulted in the adoption of training and hardening techniques virtually unknown in all but a few armies throughout the world. During training, Japanese soldiers were often forced to undertake gruelling 80km (50 mile) marches or endure all sorts of hardships in both battle and in training well beyond the normal limits of human endurance. While Western armies trained their soldiers to be tough in battle, there still existed in these same armies self-imposed limits as to training, based on the perceived endurance levels of their soldiers. This was not the case in the Japanese Army. Japanese soldiers were expected to accept such hardships and training with unhesitating obedience. According to the code of the warrior, there were no limits to human endurance and, with *hara*, one could 'go on forever'. From this doctrine

Below: A dead Japanese soldier lies in a field in the Philippines, having killed himself with his own bayonet to avoid capture. According to his code of conduct, each Japanese soldier was expected to fight to extinction or take his own life.

Above: During the fighting in Burma in 1942, Japanese soldiers search a captured British soldier for weapons. According to Japanese beliefs, Allied prisoners had disgraced themselves by surrendering, and consequently many were harshly treated.

prisoners of war, one Japanese officer told his captors at the end of the war: 'Our men had no special instructions beforehand. But when prisoners came in, we instructed the troops to send them back to headquarters without injuring them. I think that although war is inhuman, we must act as humanely as possible. When I took some of your men [British soldiers] prisoner in Burma I gave them food and tobacco.' Hence treatment of prisoners varied in terms of when, where and how they were captured, since, as one historian has written, 'few troops feel particularly tender when they have just come through a battle'. On the other hand, the majority of Japanese soldiers saw surrender as a means of disgrace and thus unforgivable.

In short, the samurai saw themselves as the true patriots of Japan, defenders of the throne and of the nation itself. The code of the warrior meant that diplomacy was viewed as a sign of weakness, and the notion that problems be settled accordingly was therefore detested. During the interwar era, this feeling came to the fore, as the most vociferous opponents of disarmament came from the military establishments in the Army and Navy. These same military men saw disarmament as a means of taking away their occupations. As a result, both secret and open societies sought to 'purify' national life through increased militarisation. One such open society was the *Sakura-kai* (Cherry Society), which was formed by the officers in the Manchurian Kwangtung Army and openly opposed any withdrawal from Manchuria or the unification of China under Chiang Kai-shek.

Secret societies included those formed by individuals, mostly fanatical young officers inside both the Army and Navy, who were opposed to any peaceful overture to the West. This group, known as the Imperial Way, conducted a self-imposed programme of terror aimed at senior officers, diplomats and civilians deemed disloyal to the Emperor and his army. These young officers, committed to territorial expansion, in turn issued 'The Great Purpose', which summed up their views towards the Emperor and the *Hakko-Ichi-u*: 'With due reverence, we consider that the basis of the divinity of our country lies in the fact that the nation is destined to expand under the Imperial Rule until it embraces the world.'

Yet there existed a contradiction in the term 'nation', as understood by the West: Japan as a nation did not exist until after the Restoration in 1868. This was when the Emperor, the clans and the people became linked as a single political entity. As the nineteenth century ended, clan loyalty eventually gave way to that of loyalty to the

been identified as an extreme form of Western chivalry, it does not recognise the protection of either women or children, as Japanese society remained patriarchal. In fact, the samurai had complete power over women of his household and his interests remained paramount. This explains the Japanese enslavement of women as prostitutes during World War II. These 'comfort women', as they were referred to by Japanese military authorities, were at the complete mercy of their captors and were fully exploited by enlisted men and officers alike. This chauvinism likewise explains the ease with which Japanese soldiers killed innocent civilians throughout the conquered territories during World War II.

Insofar as captured British, American or other Allied prisoners of war had been concerned, the code of *Bushido* did not explicitly tell Japanese soldiers how to treat a captured enemy soldier. While it has been assumed that the Japanese soldier never quite understood the Western concept of surrender, treatment of captured Allied soldiers ranged from civility to that of bestiality. Concerning how the Japanese treated Allied

Emperor and country, thereby laying the groundwork for State Shintoism and a sense of national patriotism based on the Western concept of nationalism.

Clan Loyalty

The Japanese Army (and to a lesser degree the Navy) still, however, clung to the samurai tradition of loyalty to the clan, and with that came the development of a subculture based on militarism. Much like Confucian society in China, the Japanese Army remained committed to the teachings of loyalty to one's clan, which in time manifested itself to refer exclusively to that of the Army.

In time, a sense of 'community' grew up in the Army, with the soldier's company, battalion, and finally regiment taking the place of the civilian-based community. Each had its own laws and regulations, and was headed by the regimental commander, usually a colonel, who became a de facto chieftain, or *daimyo,* of feudal times. Hence both patriotism in the Western sense and the feudal loyalty to one's clan contributed to the growth in the Japanese Army of what is commonly referred to as *esprit de corps.* Much like in the days of the feudal chieftains, the Japanese soldier fought and fought hard due to his sense of loyalty to the Emperor, and not solely as a result of loyalty to the physical country of Japan itself. In fact, from the day that

a soldier entered the barracks of his regiment as a recruit, his superiors constantly reminded him that 'to die on the battlefield for the Emperor' was the highest possible honour a soldier could hope to obtain. Placed in the context of its Confucian antecedent, the Japanese soldier was reminded that 'death is lighter than a feather; but duty is heavier than a mountain …' With this in mind, Japanese soldiers were constantly reminded that loyalty to the Emperor was at the foundation of their service.

Thus, in order to understand the fighting motivation of the Japanese soldier in battle during World War II, it must always be kept in mind that he was driven more by a sense of loyalty than any willingness to die, and it was this loyalty which gave him the impetus to fight as hard as he did. While loyalty became obscured in the code of the warrior, due mainly to Japan's embrace of the Western concept of patriotism and the nation, it nonetheless remained a very important force which drove the Japanese armies forward during World War II, and one that kept them fighting against overwhelming odds.

Below: 'War without Mercy.' Japanese infantrymen in Indonesia bayoneting Indonesian rebels captured in early 1942. Many natives were mistreated under Japanese rule: men were forced to work as slave labourers, while women were made to sleep with soldiers.

CHAPTER 2

Recruitment, Conscription and Training

The Japanese army in 1941 was a battle-hardened force with equipment comparable to that of the future Allies in the Pacific theatre. Trained intensively, and with years of experience in Manchuria, the Japanese soldier was prepared to fight in climatic extremes, and was constantly looking to attack the enemy.

ALONGSIDE THE 'SPIRITUAL' and psychological preparedness of the Japanese soldier during the interwar era and throughout World War II, the recruitment, conscription and training of a 'Heavenly Warrior' remained paramount to sustaining the Japanese soldier during this period. The process that turned the Japanese soldier into the excellent fighter that he was took place, as it did in most Western armies, during the interwar era. In fact, as this chapter will illustrate, it was from 1919 to 1937 that the Japanese Army underwent a swift modernisation process that transformed it from an army that thought solely in terms of the 'bayonet' to one capable of fighting a fully mechanised, combined-arms battle.

RECRUITMENT AND CONSCRIPTION

Even before a Japanese soldier entered the Army, he had already undergone years of inculcation as a warrior for the Emperor. In Japan, primarily after the Restoration in 1868, military indoctrination took place from infancy. Formal regimentation and training began at about the age of eight when, starting with the third year of primary school or the third grade, all males were given semi-military training by

Left: Japanese civilians bow in reverence as Emperor Hirohito's motorcade passes by. The cult of the emperor was strong in Japan, despite the fact that power in the country was, in fact, wielded by the premier.

their teachers, who themselves were primarily former military men or reservists. Those going on to middle school, higher school, college or university then received further military training under the tutelage of Regular Army officers. From the end of the Russo–Japanese War in 1905 up to the eve of Japan's involvement in World War II in 1941, this amounted to anywhere from two or more hours per week of training, with four to six days devoted to annual manoeuvres. As time went on, the subject matter became increasingly orientated towards purely military subjects. Those youths who did not elect to further their education continued their training in what were called youth schools, or *Seinen Gakko*, set up by the government to reinforce their primary school military training. Special emphasis was given to training paratroops and to aviation-related subjects. In time, the government added numerous courses of a purely military nature in order to turn the middle schools into training camps for cadets, and the universities and higher schools into military academies to train reserve officers and NCOs.

The basis for the Japanese conscription and recruitment systems dated back to before World War I, when German advisers introduced these systems during the last two decades of the nineteenth century. In theory, all eligible males between the ages of 17 and 40 years old could be called to serve, although in reality this never occurred, as the average age of the Japanese soldier was 20 years old. During the Russo–Japanese War (1904–1905), all young men aged 20 were examined by a Council of Reform in each town or village. All eligible recruits averaging 1.52m (5ft) or more in height were then divided into three categories. The first class of conscript normally served two years of active service, the first class of reserve four years and four months, the second class of reserves 10 years, and, finally, the territorial reserve 17 years and 4 months.

Conscripts serving in the second class, or *Hojuhei*, were assigned to a special formation called 'conscript reserves', similar in training to the German pre-World War I *Ersatz* organisation and system of training. Unlike those assigned to the first two categories of active and first-class reserve service, the second-class reservists underwent only a short period of training. Recruits assigned to the third class of reserves went immediately into the territorial reserve. Those recruits who fell under the required height of 1.52m (5ft) and averaged in height at around 1.4m (4ft 7in), or were unable to meet the annual call-up due to injury or illness, were immediately assigned to the territorial reserves until the next year's call-up. At that time, they were either accepted for service or permanently rejected. Thus, only a portion of those eligible for call-up served at any one time. Those men who were classified as either unfit for military service or who were between the ages of 37 and 40, as well as teenagers aged from 17 to 20, were automatically placed into the national army conscript category, or *Kokuminhei*. While men falling into this category received little, if any, training, they nonetheless were liable for service in an extreme emergency. As World War II drew to a close, like its German ally, the Japanese Army began to rely on this body of manpower to fill the ranks and possibly to assist in the defence of the Home Islands themselves in the event of an Allied landing.

During the interwar era, the average strength of the Japanese Army stood at around 300,000 officers and men.

Below: A Sumo wrestler instructs Japanese schoolchildren in martial arts. This was an essential element in preparing Japanese boys for military service, and all schoolchildren received semi-military training from the age of eight.

During the time of call-up for military service, which was in January of every year, the Japanese Army normally stood at an annual strength of 500,000 conscripts and 100,000 men from those temporarily rejected the previous year. After undergoing a prearranged period of initial or recruit training – which lasted approximately six months and consisted of physical training, bayonet training, field training, company and platoon tactics, forced marching, close order drill, musketry and the inculcation of the soldier's code, or *Senjinkun* – the recruits then passed on to advanced training. This training was carried out by either veteran NCOs or company-grade officers, usually captains and lieutenants. The Japanese soldier, whether a commissioned officer or enlisted man, was taught from the outset that he was expected to endure all types of hardships and that he should therefore live a Spartan life. His food was simple, as were his living conditions, which were extremely puritanical.

After completing this training, the Japanese soldier was assigned to a permanent regiment. Much like the German regimental system, the newly arrived recruit received additional military training in the barracks square of his assigned company. Here, the soldier was acquainted with all aspects of the duties and responsibilities of being a warrior for the Emperor. Charged with this training were career-serving NCOs and officers, primarily company grade officers (captains, first and second lieutenants or subalterns), who further instilled a sense of loyalty into the

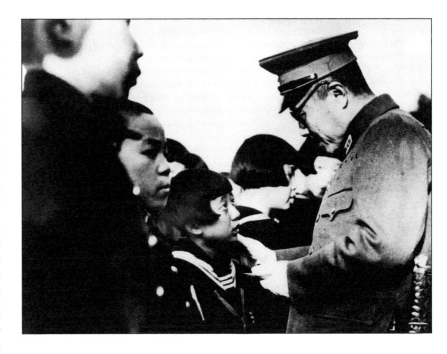

Above: Japanese premier General Tojo talks with children whose fathers were killed fighting the Chinese in Manchuria in 1943. Note that these children are already in uniforms of their own, ready to follow their fathers in serving the emperor.

soldier, with the greatest attention being paid to the seven military values of loyalty, valour, patriotism, obedience, humility, morality and honour. Japanese Army training during this era can be summed up as progressive in nature and was one that was both tough and demanding on the individual soldier.

At the end of June of every year, the regiment left the barracks and carried out company-, battalion-, regimental-, brigade- and, finally, divisional-level training. This training culminated in the annual autumn manoeuvres, where as

JAPANESE ARMY CONSCRIPT TRAINING	
Period	Type of Training
January to May	Recruit Training. This included general instruction in squad (section) training, bayonet training and target practice. In February, a march of five days with bivouacking at night was held to train men to endure the cold.
June and July	Target practice, field works, platoon and company training and bayonet training. Marching 32km (20 miles) per day.
August	Company and battalion training, field work, combat firing, swimming and bayonet fighting. Marching 40km (25 miles) per day.
October to November	Battalion and regimental training. Combat firing. Autumn manoeuvres.

Above: Japanese civilians were required to undertake military training both before and during World War II. Here women and young boys practise fire safety techniques in case of bomb attack in a cloud of smoke and spray.

period of training (shortened during World War II) at one of the NCO schools (*Kyodo Gakko*) or at one of the Army branch schools or service schools. NCOs (*Kashikan*), many of whom who had made the Army a career, included first sergeants, sergeants and corporals. Each NCO had extensive service within the Army or had been highly trained for a particular branch. Each one also had equal responsibility in training the men under his care, as did the officers.

Apprentice System

In order to meet the demand for highly trained technicians and other specialists, the Army adopted an apprentice system (*Rikugun Shonenhei*). Youths from 14 to 15 years of age were recruited and given basic military training before being inducted into the Army as what the Japanese Army officials called 'youth soldiers'. After a probationary period of six months, these young soldiers, given the rank of superior private (private first class) or lance-corporal, were then promoted to the rank of corporal after graduation from a branch school. These youth soldiers then attended their particular branch school, primarily in the fields of aviation, signals, tank, artillery and ordnance.

During the 1920s, the *Seinendan* (youth training centres) became an important source of trained manpower.

many as from two to eight divisions participated. These manoeuvres were very strenuous and included a great deal of forced marching with full field packs or kits. These forced marches averaged 50–65km (30–40 miles) a day and were undertaken in sunshine or rain, at night and during the day. Great emphasis was placed upon successfully completing the march.

Neither the officer nor the enlisted man enjoyed much in the way of relaxation and little time was given to the playing of sports. While officers engaged in two-handed fencing, with a two-handed bamboo sword, enlisted men participated in bayonet fighting, ju-jitsu and wrestling. The two-handed fencing conducted by the officers dated back to feudal times and consisted mainly of cutting. Officers who participated in this exercise wore body armour made of lacquered wood, an iron grill mask and gauntlets (so that they resembled a modern-day baseball catcher), as one could be severely injured or killed if struck by an opponent. All of these exercises, for both officers and enlisted men, were undertaken and encouraged by Army officials in order to foster aggressiveness and team work.

NCOs in the Japanese Army came from conscripts who had served three months' active service in the Army and received an additional nine months of special training with troops, whereupon they became NCO candidates known as *Kashikan Kohosha*. They were then given a one-year

Below: More than 50,000 students from the Tokyo, Kanagana, Saitama and Chiba prefectures, dressed in military uniforms, parade in front of the Meiji shrine before going off to fight alongside their elders on 21 October 1943.

JAPANESE ARMY 'YOUTH' SOLDIERS' TRAINING

School	Length
Shonen Tsushinhei (Signal)	Two years at the Army Youth Signal School
Shonen Senshahei (Tank)	Two years at the Army Youth Tank School located near Mount Fuji
Shonen Hohei (Artillery)	Two years at the Army Field Artillery School or the Army Air Defence School
Ordnance	Two-year course at the Army's Ordnance School
Shonen Hikohei (Aviation)	The usual course lasted three years. After one year at a general aviation course in Tokyo, students were divided into three groups: pilots, who attended school at Utsunomiya or Kumagi; signalmen, who went to the Air Signals School; and mechanics, who attended school at Tokorozawa or Gifu. They spent two years at one of these special schools, the last as youth soldiers. Those youths possessing special skills went either directly to flying school at Tachiarai or to maintenance school at Gifu.

These centres – established by Prime Minister Tanaka Giichi and Army Minister General Ugaki Kazushige, both classmates at the Japanese War College, in unison with the Minister for Education Okada Ryohei – further militarised the education of Japanese youth. Army drill instructors were now sent to middle schools to instil patriotism, physical fitness and loyalty among Japan's burgeoning male population. By mid-July 1926, the youth training centres were in full operation.

Initially, they were administered and financed by the Education Ministry, with approximately 40,000 of the 110,00 instructors being Army Reservists (officers and NCOs). Students were required to undertake about 400 hours of Army drill. Local Army regimental commanders were responsible for inspecting the state of the student's military proficiency. From 1926 until the end of World War II, the Army worked through both the youth training centres and education ministry in order to train future officers and NCOs. These centres were located throughout the Home Islands in major Army districts of administration, in order to coordinate and facilitate the activities of the local regimental commanders.

The Japanese Army likewise used the centres for military drill and patriotic training, and the youth association branches for broader military, physical and patriotic training, in order to maintain strong army–community ties. This relationship enabled the Army to recruit students for the youth training centres. In time, some communities went so far as to relinquish their drill responsibilities to the *Seinendan*.

As for the numbers of Japanese youths trained in the *Seinendan*s, figures show that, during their first year of operation, they trained more than 800,000 male teenagers, with the numbers growing steadily from then on. By 1934, more than one-third, or 915,000, of Japan's young men in the appropriate age bracket studied and drilled at these youth training centres. It is not surprising, therefore, that by the time a Japanese soldier entered basic training, he was already accustomed to military life.

Throughout the course of training, special attention was given to the inculcation of 'morale' or spiritual instruction. Japanese officers often read the Imperial Rescript to Soldiers (issued by the Emperor Meiji on 4 January 1882) to the enlisted men and constantly emphasised the seven principles of military ethics.

As for the length of training, first and second conscript reserves underwent a six-month period of training. The training was not as intensive as that given to active service men, but it did attempt to cover, in a relatively short period of time, all that the active service men learned in their two-year course. During peacetime, men who had served their requisite two years of active service with the Army or *Genekihei*, and had subsequently been relegated to the First Reserve, were required to undergo further military training from time to time during their period of liability. During World War II, the subsequent drain on trained manpower ended the minimum periods of training. This meant that Japanese recruits were literally sent directly from the training depots to the front lines, where they received on-the-job training. Even during peacetime, however, Japanese Army conscripts received the bulk of their training in operational areas. This was particularly true in China and Manchuria, where the Japanese High Command used both theatres to train their men in various combat skills. Often, recruits sent to operational theatres either remained in garrison or, in some instances, were sent into the field to experience actual combat during their period of training.

During wartime, the Japanese soldier served what Western armies called 'for the duration', although technically service had been extended from the pre-war two-year stint to a wartime length of three years. Certain individuals who possessed a technical or specialist skill were often granted deferments, especially those who worked in the airplane, ordnance or munitions factories. In order to make up this deficit, the Japanese Army began to draft Koreans (from 1944) and Taiwanese (in early 1945). While the Japanese employed a few of these colonial conscripts as combat troops against Allied forces during World War II, the vast majority of them served as military labourers and were thus given little, if any, combat training. In the case of the Koreans, it is interesting to note that many of the post-World War II Republic of Korea military leaders actually trained as Japanese Army officers in Manchuria. As for Taiwan, the Japanese managed to conscript approximately 315,000 natives, although few, if any, served in the actual war, as it ended before they could be trained to fight.

Below: Preparing for Armageddon. Japanese civilians undergo military training as American armies prepare for an invasion of the Japanese homeland. These civilians are drilling with bamboo spears in readiness for hand-to-hand combat.

NCOs or *Kashikans*

Like its Western counterparts, the Japanese Army prided itself on its long-term NCOs. Starting with its sergeants major (*socho*) and sergeants (*gunso*), and ending with the rank of corporal (*gocho*), Japanese NCOs received a thorough, albeit very narrow and rigid, education. Japanese Army officials aimed this education primarily at training infantry and combat arms leaders. NCOs, starting with the rank of corporal, attended one of the four NCO academies or *Kyodo Gakko*, located at Sendai, Kumamoto, Toyohashi and Kungchuling (Manchuria). These NCO academies were primarily devoted to infantry, with the exception of some schools focusing on artillery, armour, cavalry, engineering, veterinary, medical and ordnance. Normally, the NCOs attending the latter were required to have had some civilian training in either maintenance or technical skills such as mechanics, signals or telephone repair. Some of these NCOs attended one of the apprentice schools previously mentioned. Japanese NCOs likewise attended special courses at the tank School, Military Police, Medical School, the various air schools and the Mechanised Equipment Maintenance School.

OFFICER RECRUITMENT AND TRAINING

There were two classifications of Japanese officers: regular army officers and reserve officers. Separate to this were the special volunteer officers known as *Tokubetsu Shigan Shoko* and warrant officers known as *Junshikans*. The regular and reserve officers fell into three distinct types of officers: (a) those who graduated from the full course at the Japanese Military Academy; (b) those who obtained commissions either through the reserve officer's candidate course after having served in the ranks or direct from a technical institution; and (c) former warrant officers and NCOs who had risen from the ranks. No matter where they came from, all Japanese officers, both regular and reserve, served a probationary period that lasted from two to six months after the completion of their training.

Regular Army officers were further broken down according to their training. Those Japanese males who graduated from the main Military

Academy (the Japanese version of Sandhurst or West Point) or the Air Academy usually entered the line branches such as the infantry, artillery, cavalry, armour and aviation units. The graduates of the technical and scientific schools and institutes served in the support and technical services. Most of these officers had been selected prior to entering the Army and had been students when chosen for a particular branch. They were usually educated at government expense at specified universities and colleges offering a particular curriculum. University graduates received their commissions as first lieutenants.

The third category included selected warrant and NCOs in active service under 38 years of age, who became candidates for commissions. These officers were known officially as *Shoi Kohosha* and received a one-year course of instruction at the Military Academy, the Air Academy, the Military Police School or one of the Army schools. In peacetime, they rarely advanced beyond the rank of captain, as they were so close to retirement age.

Reserve officers were made up of Class A reserve officer candidates (*Koshu Kambu Kohosei*) who met the requirements

Above: Camouflaged Japanese infantry advance to the front line along a river rather than force a path through dense jungle in Burma. Well trained in this environment, the Japanese soldier was an excellent jungle fighter.

of regular officers. They were drawn primarily from regular army conscripts who had certain educational qualifications (mostly two years of high school). After three months of intensive training with their respective units, they became candidates; after a further three months training, they were classified by examination into 'A' candidates (those suitable for officer commissions) and 'B' candidates (those suitable to be appointed as NCOs).

After having been selected, the A candidates were then sent to one of the regular courses for reserve officer candidates. Upon receiving a peacetime commission, they were placed into the reserves by Army officials. From this point, they were called into active service (known as *Shoshu Shoko*). It is important to note that during World War II it was from this category that the bulk of Japanese officers would come.

The special volunteer officers (*Tokubetsu Shigan Shoko*) came primarily from field and company grade officers (second lieutenant to colonel), and had been permitted to volunteer for active service for a period of two years, and for one-year periods after that, up to retirement age. During World War II, this designation was given to all young reserve officer candidates after they had served a probationary period with troops. Special volunteer officers often qualified for a one-year course at the Military Academy. Successful completion of this course would entitle them to become volunteer regular officers and also offered them the possibility of rising to the rank of major in the Regular Japanese Army.

The last category of officers came from the warrant officers, or *Junshikans*. These were selected by the promotion of qualified NCOs, and came primarily from the technical fields, as well as combat support (artillery, cavalry, tanks, medicine and signal branches). The actual training of a young officer was as rigid as, if not more so than, that of an ordinary soldier. Besides the emphasis on infantry tactics, field problems, drill and swordsmanship, the officer candidate received a heavy amount of indoctrination training. Above all else, Japanese officers were taught from the outset that their position on the battlefield was always in front of the troops.

Like Western armies during the same era, the Japanese military authorities endeavoured to insure that officers were of appropriate age for their respective grades. Minimum time limits in grade were established as follows:

Below: Japanese soldiers wearing gas masks during pre-war training. The Japanese had undertaken extensive testing of chemical weapons, both in the lab and at training grounds, and fully expected gas to be used against them.

from sublieutenant (subaltern or second lieutenant) to lieutenant and from lieutenant to captain was two years; captain to major, four years; major to lieutenant-colonel, three years; lieutenant-colonel to colonel and colonel to brigadier-general, two years; brigadier-general to major-general, four years. Corps commanders and field marshals were personally selected by the Emperor. To this end, age limits were established to ensure the ability and fitness required for Army officers. The maximum age for field officers and general officers was 50 years for majors, 53 years for lieutenant-colonels, 55 years for colonels, 58 years

Above: Japanese soldiers on skis in Manchuria during 1937. During training, soldiers were sent on long marches in the snow and expected to bivouac in freezing temperatures in order to condition them to the harsh conditions.

for brigadier-generals, 62 years for major-generals and 65 years for corps commanders. There was no prescribed limit for field marshals.

FIELD AND WEAPONS TRAINING

Japanese Army infantry training progressed from the smallest unit, the squad (section), to platoon, company, battalion and regimental training, and culminated in combined manoeuvres at the end of every year. During the second year of duty, training was similar in scope, but with more time devoted to specialist training in the respective branch to which a soldier might find himself assigned. As for the quality of this training, Japanese infantry training was progressive and gradualistic in process, growing in both intensity and scope. Japanese soldiers conducted long marches with full equipment and endured stiff endurance tests; military officials considered these necessary to produce in the soldier the ability to withstand hunger and fatigue for long periods.

One myth that requires clarification is the long-held belief that the Japanese soldier was a good jungle fighter. While the statement in itself is true, the fact remained that the Japanese infantryman had been trained to fight in all climates and places, a factor that dominated his conditioning while training. Furthermore, if anything, the

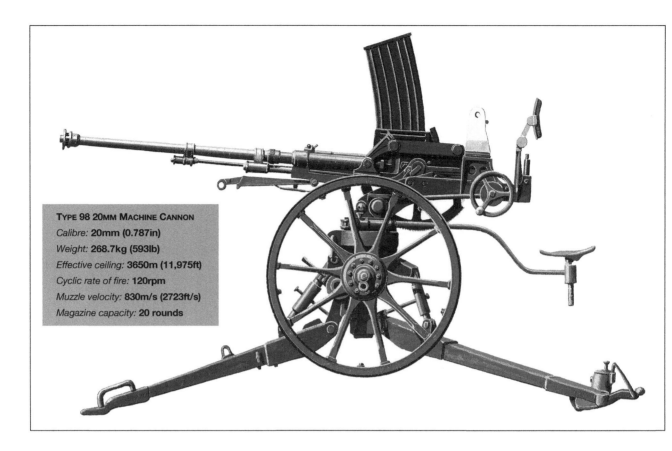

TYPE 98 20MM MACHINE CANNON
Calibre: **20mm (0.787in)**
Weight: **268.7kg (593lb)**
Effective ceiling: **3650m (11,975ft)**
Cyclic rate of fire: **120rpm**
Muzzle velocity: **830m/s (2723ft/s)**
Magazine capacity: **20 rounds**

Japanese soldier had been trained to fight primarily what would be termed a conventional war, much in the style of the Western Front during World War I. Indeed, the fighting techniques employed by the Japanese soldier during World War II, particularly during the long war in China, had first been used during the Russo–Japanese War of 1904–05.

Japanese soldiers were trained to endure all types of hardships, in all climates and over all types of terrain. Most important was the training in mountain- and cold weather warfare, carried out in northern Japan, Korea and on Formosa (Taiwan). There, Japanese infantrymen conducted what were called *setchu kogun*, or 'snow marches'. These marches, which lasted four to five days, were normally conducted towards the end of January or during the first week in February, when the weather in northern Japan was at its coldest. As part of the hardening process, Japanese soldiers on sentry duty were not permitted to wear gloves, while bivouacking was carried out at night and in the open. The main objective of this conditioning was to accustom both officers and enlisted men to the cold. During July and August, Japanese soldiers were sent on long conditioning marches in order to accustom them to the heat. In these and other ways, Japanese troops were trained to endure extremes of temperature, basic living conditions and hardships of all kinds.

As a means of reinforcing this Spartan existence, the Japanese diet and accommodations were both simple and practical. The Japanese soldier's diet normally consisted of a large bowl of rice, a cup of green tea, a plate of Japanese pickles, smoked fish and fried bean paste or some other local delicacy, such as fruits and vegetables. The Japanese mess room consisted of a large, plain table with wooden benches mounted on an uncarpeted, planked wooden floor. Usually, a large banner or script was posted that exhorted loyalty to the Emperor or listed one of the seven military virtues.

As to the types of training the Japanese infantrymen underwent, it is sufficient to say that it was both varied and thorough. Japanese officers maintained, however, that soldiers trained in the outlying garrisons in the country received better field training than did those stationed in urban areas. At Wakamtsu, for instance, in the countryside, the terrain was ideal for varied tactical manoeuvres, night marches, field firing with live ammunition, exercises in fording rivers, building bridges, bivouacking, trench construction and other important training that soldiers could not undergo in the city due to restrictions on the available terrain for training.

Nonetheless, there was both uniformity in method and purpose in the training of a Japanese soldier, all of which better prepared him for war. This included training in such areas as bayonet fighting, camouflage, patrolling, night manoeuvres, musketry, marching, field hygiene and sanitation, first aid and military innovation. Broken down individually, each aspect in the training of a Japanese soldier for war was designed to prepare the infantryman for modern twentieth-century warfare, while at the same time, maintaining the code of *Bushido*.

Bayonet Training

Above all else, Japanese military authorities stressed bayonet training. In fact, Japanese infantrymen were taught from the beginning of their training that the bayonet was the weapon of the infantry and that with it, and only with it, could the enemy be forced to give ground. The individual soldier was constantly reminded by his officers and NCOs that the ultimate result is sought in the assault and that the bayonet is the ultimate factor in every assault. Because the 'spirit' of the Japanese Army was the spirit of the offensive, Japanese infantry instructors repeatedly emphasised that the bayonet was 'essentially the weapon of the offensive'. To ensure the soldier was effective in its use, Japanese manuals stressed that the infantryman must be 'confident,

skilled and without fear, and that … he must have absolute confidence in his weapon and in himself.' With this in mind, Japanese infantry constantly trained and practised in the nurturing of the 'spirit of the bayonet'. A large part of the instruction in bayonet training was devoted to personal combat. Here, the spirit of ju-jitsu, or mind over matter, came into play, as the Japanese soldier was constantly reminded that in battle he must often defeat man after man until he himself is either defeated or killed by his enemy. In order to promote defeat of the enemy with the bayonet, Japanese bayonet instructors – usually civilian bayonet and sword fencing masters – stressed the long thrust to the exclusion of all other forms of attack, while the butt of the rifle was seldom, if ever, concentrated upon. Japanese soldiers were taught that, if the first long thrust failed, they were to drop their rifles and close with the enemy, using their hands and feet. Likewise, in combat, there is no time for fencing with an opponent, so the Japanese soldier was

Below: Japanese Type 94 Tankettes parade down a main avenue in China during World War II. Contrary to popular opinion, the Japanese army in 1941 was more prepared for fighting a mechanised war against China or Russia than fighting in jungles.

encouraged to aim first for the abdomen and then for the throat. The attack was to be made in pairs as far as possible. As the Japanese soldier became skilled in night fighting, his instructors stressed the use of the bayonet. To this end, night manoeuvres were carried out with unsheathed bayonets in order to accustom the men to handling the rifle in darkness.

Due largely to the lessons learned during the Russo–Japanese War, as well as World War I, Japanese soldiers were taught offensive and defensive trench warfare tactics, which included use of the bayonet. Here, trainers developed what they called a 'trench run', which was essentially a trench dug approximately 3.65m (12ft) deep and 2.44m (8ft) wide, across which soldiers were required to charge. One soldier was to bend over, while his companions leapt upon his back and scrambled over the top with their rifles still held in their right hands. The sides of the trench had a slope of about three degrees, revetted with a series of poles interwoven with reeds in order for the soldiers to use as a grip to exit the trench in a hurry.

Below: Japanese troops cooking a meal before the next battle. The infantryman's usual meal was a large bowl of rice supplemented with pickles and fried bean paste. Local food supplies, such as fresh fish, were a welcome change.

Once the soldier exited the first trench line, he then proceeded to the next one, where he met a belt of barbed wire about 15m (50ft) deep. The job of the first three men to reach the wire – which was about 1m (3ft) in height – was to throw themselves as far forwards into the wire as possible and begin cutting it from the bottom. They could then crawl underneath the wire as they cleared a path for their comrades. The first man to throw himself over the wire was to lay his rifle over it in front of him, while the man proceeding him leapt on the back of the former onto the rifle, and from there on, deeper into the wire. This method was repeatedly used by Japanese soldiers during World War II, particularly when there was no artillery support to clear enemy barbed wire. Storming barbed wire in this fashion reduced the time necessary to cut through the first 4.5m (15ft) of enemy wire.

The emphasis on bayonet training was extended to all categories of Japanese conscripts and reserves. In fact, even students in high schools, colleges and universities who reported for their annual three weeks of military duty with their regiment received a considerable amount of bayonet training. At least an hour and a half each day in the training schedule of a Japanese soldier revolved around use of the bayonet and a series of personal combats; at least another 30 minutes was given to instruction on the bayonet run, where students and regular soldiers alike practised bayonet assaults over broken terrain, through barbed wire and over other such obstacles.

Musketry Training

Musketry training in the Japanese Army was aimed primarily at NCOs, who were charged with the application of the principles of collective rifle fire in battle. In collective rifle fire, the teamwork could be exceptional, although the accuracy of the individual soldier decreased rapidly at ranges over 264m (300yd). Japanese NCOs were trained in the estimation of ranges by eyesight and thoroughly familiarised with the conditions that affected the appearance of targets, such as light and terrain, background, depressions, darkness, and climatic conditions such as rain, cloud cover and fog. They likewise received careful training in the estimation of distance by the observation of fire. In China and in Manchuria, where the ground was dry and usually dusty, training in range estimation proved very effective, as rifle fire often found its target. In addition to training in rifle fire, Japanese heavy machine-gunners were schooled in the use of range cards when their unit was on the defence.

During World War II, Japanese soldiers were not known for their accuracy in shooting at individual targets,

Above: Japanese soldiers seek cover in Shanghai, China, in 1942, well prepared for a poison gas attack. The Japanese soldier was extensively trained in the use of gas masks while in combat since gas had been regularly used on the Western Front in World War I.

but were said to be more effective in hitting moving targets. This was where Japanese musketry training had placed its greatest emphasis during advanced infantry training before the advent of war in the 1930s. An added feature of Japanese marksmanship training was in the use of surprise targets; soldiers were likewise taught to fire by sections, so increasing the probability of hits. A normal Japanese Army rifle section consisted of two rifle squads and a light machine-gun squad. The six sections of both peace- and wartime-strength rifle companies were organised to bring the maximum firepower to bear against the enemy.

Scouting and Patrolling

Scouting and patrolling were heavily emphasised during training and in war. In fact, one US Army observer with the Japanese Army during the 1920s wrote: 'scouting and patrolling in the Japanese Army has been reduced to an exact science in which no detail is too minute to be overlooked or slighted either by instructors or pupils in practice or by scouts and patrols in time of war.'

This same US Army observer noted that small stature and excellent eyesight made the Japanese soldier extremely efficient in scouting and patrolling. Individual scouts received very careful training in their duties. In fact, only the most intelligent men of a section were trained as scouts. As this same observer noted, however, Japanese scouts were poorly trained in such skills as map-reading and sketching. While critics noted that these were essential skills for a scout, Japanese training emphasised actual observation of the enemy in determining his position, strength, rates of march and what arms of service and wheeled vehicles the enemy force had in its possession, rather than map-reading. As the Japanese Army demonstrated in Burma and in the South-west Pacific, particularly on Guadalcanal, New Britain and New Guinea, its scouts proved to be second to none, as they consistently outmanoeuvred their British, American and Australian pursuers. In fact, Japanese soldiers were known throughout the Pacific War to possess a keen sense of observation, and the Army took special pride in its systematic training in observation techniques and the development of the natural abilities of the ordinary soldier in this area.

Japanese scouts were trained always to reconnoitre to the front and flanks of assaulting platoons, although they were not used when platoons were ordered to flank an enemy point of resistance. The thinking here was that the use of scouts in this type of operation was more likely to tip off the enemy and thus negate the element of surprise. Thus, they would rather move forwards by scout reconnaissance. In the scout's training. special emphasis was given to the need to transmit information to the rear at once that would seem to indicate movement on the part of the enemy, such as preparations for a counter-attack. Scouts were also instructed to report when the assault units were held up or driven back, or when any enemy breakthrough occurred in the assaulting unit's lines.

All scouts were masters of camouflage. Each army scout carried his own green netting, which he filled with grass, weeds, branches or twigs of trees and then threw over his head to provide all-round cover and concealment. Japanese soldiers were trained to use the surrounding terrain to determine the most effective means of camouflage protection. With the aid of such cover and concealment, Japanese scouts were reportedly trained to penetrate to within 27m (30yd) of an enemy's frontline positions without being observed. In this area of camouflage, the Japanese soldier was trained to take advantage of any surrounding grass or scrub brush.

As for patrolling techniques, Japanese soldiers received excellent training which emphasised teamwork above all else. In fact, teamwork between members of a Japanese Army patrol was said to be excellent. Soldiers were taught to move out in single file or as a line of skirmishers. Unlike American patrolling methods, the use of the 'diamond' technique was discouraged, nor did Japanese patrols divide into two parallel columns as US Marines practised and used in the Caribbean and in Nicaragua in the 1920s. Patrol formations were, in fact, usually quite compact

Below: Japanese soldiers and tanks prepare for combat. Tanks were rarely used in mass formations in World War II by the Japanese; they were usually found in small numbers acting as mobile pillboxes in support of the infantry.

when moving through woods or villages. The patrol leader was always on 'point' or at the head of the column with no rear guard. Another important factor was that, by and large, the Japanese discouraged the use of patrols. When patrol actions were ordered, the Japanese Army had a fondness for assigning officers to lead patrols, unlike in Western armies, where a sergeant or corporal was assigned to lead such a mission. The commander of any point of any detachment of any size was always a commissioned officer. In addition, half of all combat patrols and at least one-third of all reconnaissance patrols were led by commissioned officers during World War II.

Field or 'Forced' Marching

The great stress placed upon toughness and endurance meant that the Japanese Army emphasised marching in its training programme. This was despite the numerous problems the Japanese soldier was forced to endure because of ill-fitting leather boots. On many occasions in the course of a training or combat march, a soldier would discard his boots and replace them with straw sandals, or *warsjis*, which he carried in his field pack and put on during one of many halts during the length of a forced hike.

The pace of the march was always decided upon prior to its commencement and was strictly adhered to regardless of how difficult it was to maintain. Companies remained fairly well closed up and any soldier (or officer) who fell out of a march was dealt with severely. One British observer attached to the Japanese Army during the 1920s noted that, in one instance, a Japanese officer who had fallen out due to sheer exhaustion committed suicide by *hara-kiri* in 'order to wipe out what he considered to be an irretrievable disgrace'. Company commanders usually marched in the rear of the column during a march, with either a second- or first lieutenant leading the column. Halts were conducted every 50 minutes of hiking, with a 10-minute rest thereafter in order to allow the men to change their socks or drink water.

Field Hygiene

The Japanese soldier strictly adhered to proper field sanitation. While in garrison, barracks were meticulously cleaned and blankets and bedding was aired every day. The Japanese Army moved primarily on foot, so great attention was paid to the treatment of feet, and socks were changed twice a day whenever possible. All soldiers were required to bathe, in both summer and winter, and were likewise ordered to change their underwear every or every other day. Those charged with the preparation of rations were

A Japanese private in Luzon in December 1941. He carries an Arisaka rifle and a long blade for cutting through jungle.

Above: A Japanese rifleman takes aim at Allied soldiers in the jungle. Japanese marksmanship was better when firing in a group, and, curiously, against moving targets. However, snipers would prey on any Allied troops that were pinned down.

inspected daily by their commanding officers to ensure that their hands, fingernails and clothing were kept clean.

Field Medicine

Despite the fact that Japanese soldiers often went untreated for wounds, or were left behind by their comrades, they received thorough instruction in the administration of first aid to a fallen comrade. Japanese soldiers received lectures on where arteries were located and in the application of tourniquets and other means of stopping heavy bleeding. They could also treat sprains, fractures and dislocations of bones. Japanese infantrymen likewise knew basic antidotes for snakebites and insect bites, as well as for other infectious poisons mostly associated with jungle warfare. Japanese soldiers were skilled in the correct application of bandages to wounds and knew how to prevent the wound becoming infected.

Most important, however, was the fact that the Japanese soldier knew how to deal with sunstroke. He could also improvise from the materials at hand and make a portable litter from coats, blankets, tents or other articles of clothing and equipment as the situation dictated. In short, as one US Army observer noted after witnessing a field exercise: 'The Japanese soldier had a better knowledge of first aid than the American soldier possesses.'

Rations

In the field and on the march, the Japanese soldier's ration, or *schichi bu no san*, consisted of milled wheat and rice, and apportioned to seven portions of rice to three of wheat per soldier. This was then mixed up and placed in a large cauldron or pot, and was served to the men three times a day. This was also the staple diet in garrison, although it was often supplemented with other delicacies. Japanese soldiers were given bread once a week, although this was not compulsory. In fact, Japanese soldiers, like most Asians, had little liking for bread and instead preferred to eat rice or wheat for their starch supplement. Soldiers drank green tea or hot water with all three meals.

Gas Warfare

Two important lessons learned by the Japanese from World War I was the importance of gas warfare and the subsequent necessity of being able to operate in that type of battlefield environment. In December 1926, the Japanese Army held a large three-day manoeuvre with toxic gasses at the Army's Engineer School, located 29km (12 miles) from Tokyo. According to published reports, the exercise's main aim was to test the efficiency of the offensive and defensive qualities of the different types of war gases prepared by its Army Research laboratory under field conditions.

During this exercise, the Japanese troops tested the effect of these toxic substances on various laboratory animals. Later, Army officials emphasised that the main purposes of this exercise were to not only 'improve the Japanese Army's toxic gas services' as a whole, but also to 'formulate a practical plan for the employment of chemicals in aid to and against airplanes and artillery'.

Reports formulated at the conclusion of the exercise noted that the 'results obtained in this exercise showed a marked improvement over those obtained in the recent gas maneuver' a few months earlier on 20–24 August 1926 at Asashikawa. A US Army observer reported: 'the above exercise demonstrates the fact the Japanese army possesses agents which have proved satisfactory in the laboratory, the research into which had reached the point where a field test was necessary'. The observer went on to note that 'the selection of the Army Engineer School as the place for the exercise undoubtedly was due to the fact that the school possesses considerable meteorological equipment'. It also underscored the later war concerns of the dedicated Japanese efforts to employ toxic weapons on the battlefield, especially in China.

COMBINED ARMS AND MANOEUVRES

While the Japanese Army had been organised by and large along European lines, and the lessons of World War I had been studied with keen interest, it nonetheless maintained that the lessons of the late war were inconclusive as to the value of modern arms and equipment in the attack. Much of what the Japanese had learned had been copied from the experiences of Great Britain, Germany and France, as well as from their own experiences in the Russo–Japanese War. One of the foremost characteristics of Japanese manoeuvres was the fact that they were strenuous and realistic, and that Japanese military officials demanded the best from their men at all times.

During the interwar era, when most Japanese tactical and operational doctrine was formulated, manoeuvres stressed realism. While, for the Japanese, manoeuvres remained an important part in any army's training, the 1925 and 1926 Army manoeuvres proved decisive in the Japanese Army's evolution as a modern combat force. The 1925 manoeuvres, held in late September 1925, consisted of a joint Army–Navy exercise in and around Tokyo. During this exercise, more than 60 planes, several observation balloons, 2 infantry regiments, 2 brigades of cavalry, 1 regiment of field artillery, 1 battalion of horse artillery, engineers and the automobile corps took part in one of the largest manoeuvres to date. The aim of this particular exercise

Below: A Japanese machine gunner faces the Chinese units of Chiang Kai-shek on the Chekiang front, 1943. Japanese machine guns were slow-firing and more likely to jam than their Allied counterparts, but they were well-used for defensive purposes.

Above: A Japanese infantryman crosses a hastily-constructed pontoon bridge in Shantung province, China. Many of the men supporting the bridge were themselves wounded, but held their position until the other side of the stream was taken.

generally models produced following the war with Russia, are not, as a rule, up to as high standard as post-war guns in other countries.' The observers noted with interest that certain weapons, such as tanks and motorised vehicles, were primarily of foreign design: the heavy tank used by the Japanese was the British 'C' model, while the light tanks were French Renaults. As for motor transport, Japanese forces used American motorcycles and British trucks, which were part of the tank company's organic equipment. Air planes used by the Japanese Army Air Force included Salmsons and Nieuports.

was the defence of Tokyo and the harbour from a hostile landing force. Later that same year (1–21 October), two divisions took part in joint manoeuvres. The significance of both manoeuvres was the extensive use of air power and mechanised assets, and the fact that they laid the basis for the grand manoeuvres of 1926.

By far the most significant, and perhaps the most important, manoeuvres during the interwar era were held between 19 and 21 November 1926, when two reinforced divisions opposed each other in a two-sided exercise. The exercise involved an unopposed river crossing using pontoon bridges, a meeting engagement, withdrawal to defensive positions and a pursuit that resulted in reconnaissance and development of a hostile line, followed by an attack on an enemy's position.

The most significant features of this exercise were the new weapons that appeared for the first time during the manoeuvres, pointing to the growing sophistication of the Japanese Army and the influence of World War I on Japanese Army operational doctrine. These included for the first time the use of the tank, smoke, gas, wireless telephone and tractor-drawn artillery. Also, the infantry used newer mortars, one-pounder field guns and light and heavy machine guns, all of which were comparatively new models. The US Army observers reported: 'The artillery weapons [used by the Japanese Army and during the manoeuvre],

Triangular Organisation

As for infantry organisation, the observers noted that the Japanese infantry regiment was organised on a triangular basis and consisted of three battalions of four rifle companies and one machine-gun company. These observers likewise noted that this triangular organisation, which had made its first appearance during the 1922 Army manoeuvres, had been retained. The regiment contained a mortar detachment and one-pounders, two of each gun being used by the regiment during the manoeuvres. Each rifle company was said to have six light machine guns, while the machine-gun companies had four heavy machine guns. The number of machine guns of both types and infantry guns was increased according to wartime tables of organisation. At the review conducted following the manoeuvre, the foreign observers noted that each infantry company was about 120 strong.

As for tactics, the observers noted that the Japanese infantry, when on the offensive, were characterised by a deliberate reconnaissance, an enveloping attack and inevitable counter-attack. The firing line was reinforced as rapidly as possible during the attack and the advance pushed as far forwards as possible using the bayonet. In fact, given the 'spirit of the bayonet' ingrained in every Japanese soldier, their commanders often 'rushed' into launching the assault using the bayonet charge.

Despite the overriding employment of the bayonet amongst the ranks of the Japanese Army, the employment of firepower – namely the full use of machine guns – was

Below: How it was done when not under fire – Japanese soldiers carry their field packs and equipment on their heads as they ford a river in Burma. Without such precautions their clothing could quickly disintegrate in the warm climate.

not overlooked. In fact, every effort was made during the manoeuvres to keep the machine guns, both light and heavy, well up to the front, while at the same time making good use of overhead fire.

Tank Usage

The employment of tanks during the manoeuvres took place for the first time in 1926. Using tanks in this way signalled the beginning of the Japanese Army's interest in manoeuvre warfare. It must be emphasised, however, that during the interwar era and throughout World War II, tank were used mainly in a single role in the Japanese Army, in that they focused primarily upon providing infantry support. In only as few as a handful of instances during the fighting which raged in the Pacific – specifically on Saipan in the Marianas in 1944 and on Peleliu in September 1944 – did the Japanese use tanks in massed formations. As both the manoeuvres and actions during the war indicated, problems remained with command and control. Also, another problem centred on the liaison between infantry and artillery which, the observers noted with some candour, hardly existed. These officers noted that all messages for support were sent through division headquarters to the divisional artillery group, instead of from the battalion or regimental commander. This seemingly unnecessary diversion often meant a critical delay in artillery support for the attacking troops.

Another problem centred on communications with aircraft. As in most Western armies – and certainly with the US Marines in the jungles of Haiti, the Dominican Republic and especially Nicaragua during the 1920s – the Japanese utilised the simple but dated method of colour-coded panels in order to coordinate air- and ground

Below: A part-destroyed building provides cover for a Japanese landing party during the battle for Shanghai, China, in 1942. Japanese troops performed well not just in the jungle but in urban environments and the more exposed plains and hills of China.

cooperation during an attack against an enemy. The Japanese commanders were slow to use the new technology of wireless telephones which were so effective on behalf of their enemies in their air-to-ground and ground communications in World War II.

As already mentioned, the Japanese began to employ on an experimental basis in manouevres both gas and smoke during an attack. By 1926, these elements had become standard features of Japanese military exercises. With the commencement of the manoeuvres in 1926, the Japanese began employing motor vehicles for the effective movement of both troops and artillery. Despite this dependence on vehicles, however, the Japanese infantry division retained its use of animal transport (much like the Germans did during World War II) and still was to rely on its horses to pull supplies and artillery pieces to and from the battlefield during this period.

In fact, in the Japanese Army in particular, pack animals were the rule and not the exception when it came to the transportation of equipment. These animals would be used to transport equipment such as infantry guns, machine guns and communications gear. Despite this, the Japanese seemed to be be able to cover good ground. Even though they were travelling primarily by foot and animal transport, Japanese infantry divisions were said to be able to march distances of between 48 and 65km (30 and 40 miles) per day under ideal – and even in good – conditions.

One last lesson of the 1926 manoeuvres and the interwar era as a whole was the extensive use of reserves. During these particular manoeuvres, a substantial number of reserves were used as a part of both field forces. This served to indicate how seriously the Japanese Army took the necessity of an adequately trained reserve force. During wartime, it was these troops who would become the primary source of trained manpower for the Army and other branches of the armed forces.

ONE GOAL

Each phase of the Japanese Army's preparations during the interwar era had but one goal, and this was the recruitment, conscription and preparedness of a well-trained force of

Above: A Japanese tankette on manoeuvres with infantry before 1941. The tankette's commander is using smoke either to direct his men or cover their advance. Although fast and highly mobile, the tankettes were poorly protected and lightly armed.

infantrymen. These soldiers would receive a heavy dose both of military training and military indoctrination. The process was ongoing, from elementary school through to university or college level, and this continuity of training and indoctrination was to pay off, for it would give the Japanese Army a large reservoir of trained officers and soldiers during World War II.

Inculcated during his initial periods of training with the 'spirit of the warrior', or *Bushido*, in time the Japanese soldier would become one of the best trained – and, without a doubt, one of the most fanatical – soldiers ever faced by the armies of the United States, China, Great Britain, Australia, the Soviet Union and New Zealand.

The Japanese Army remained primarily an infantry-dominated force during World War II. It must be kept in mind that it was only against the Soviet Union and China, and on some of the islands in the Central Pacific, that the Japanese used armoured and mechanised forces.

For the most part, the slugging matches that took place in Guadalcanal, Burma, New Guinea and the Central Pacific remained primarily infantry battles. It was in these battles that the Japanese soldier would prove himself to be both resourceful and tenacious, despite the odds that were stacked against him. All of this was a result of his training and the inculcation of the 'warrior's code' during the era between the wars.

CHAPTER 3

Organisation in Peace and War, 1925–1945

> The core of the Japanese division was the humble infantryman armed with a rifle. However, Japanese divisions had a structure which allowed them to operate self-sufficiently in the field for extended periods. Specialist units were also an important part of the Japanese armoury in World War II.

THE JAPANESE ARMY THAT WENT TO war in 1931 with its invasion of Manchuria had an overall strength of 198,800 officers and men, organised into 17 divisions. By the *Jiji* (edict) of 1925, the Japanese Army retained its predominant character as an infantry-based force, although it was acknowledged that the principal objective of the Japanese Army was mobile warfare. Contrary to the pre-Pearl Harbor opinion that '[t]he Jap Army was tailor-made for the Far East', it was the simple fact that it was an infantry-based force that relied very little on mechanisation, and thus was not roadbound in the same way as the American and British forces, that led to its perceived superiority in the Far East. The Japanese Army was able to move swiftly on foot through the jungles of Malaya, Burma and the South Pacific without the encumbrances of a mechanised or motorised force.

Likewise, the organisation of the Japanese Army made it ideal for jungle warfare. The basic organisations for the Japanese soldier were the company, battalion, regiment, brigade and division. These were, in fact, the primary manoeuvre elements in the Japanese Army during the entirety of World War II. Whereas the war in Europe had been dominated by armies, groups, corps and divisions, the fighting in the Pacific, from Burma to

Okinawa, remained primarily a war characterised by units no larger than divisions, regiments and battalions, and no smaller than companies and platoons. Hence the emphasis here on the individual Japanese soldier's primary unit organisations: the division, brigade, regiment, battalion, company and platoon.

The Japanese Army in the field was organised into groups of armies, area armies, such as China and Manchuria (Kwangtung), and Southern Armies, and those forces assigned to special missions not directly under the command of either the Army's or the Navy's High Command.

THE JAPANESE ARMY INFANTRY DIVISION

By far the most important field organisation in the Japanese Army was the division. The average strength of a standard division varied in size and shape throughout World War II; nevertheless, it remained at a strength of about 20,000 officers and enlisted men, and was broken down as shown in the chart below.

Organic units of the Japanese Army division exhibited various differences in organisation and strength, due largely to the fact that they performed different roles in varying types of terrain. Each Japanese division fitted into one of three categories, A being the strongest, B the standard, and C the special. This study will concentrate on the types of division most frequently encountered by the Allies during

Left: The regimental banner of No. 56 division of the Japanese army, pictured on the march by the Irrawaddy river in Burma in February 1944. The Japanese, under the leadership of General Minakami, had suffered defeat after a fierce battle.

World War II. These included the standard division, the strengthened or 'modified' division, and the special division that was found in the Philippines and China, and was charged with counter-guerrilla operations.

The standard division was by far encountered most frequently in present operational areas. Its composition included those units and attachments mentioned below. The strengthened or 'modified' division was

Above: Japanese soldiers advancing towards a Chinese position in 1938. They wear a mixture of steel helmets and caps. The rifleman was the core of a Japanese division, most soldiers being equipped with the Arisaka rifle.

JAPANESE ARMY INFANTRY DIVISION
1941–1945

- Division headquarters
- Divisional signal units
- Infantry group headquarters and three
    infantry regiments
- Artillery regiment
- Cavalry regiment or reconnaissance regiment
- Engineer regiment
- Medical unit
- Field hospital
- Water purification unit
- Transport regiment
- Ordnance unit
- Veterinary unit

the forerunner of the strengthened division rarely encountered by Allied forces. This 'modified' division included an artillery group, but had no organic tank element or gas decontamination unit. The infantry rifle companies were found without the heavy weapons platoons of the strengthened division type, which in turn had a decreased strength in its rifle companies (262 and 205 men, respectively). In such cases, the heavy machine guns and anti-tank rifles were found in the machine gun- and anti-tank companies.

The last type of division – the special division – was a lighter type of division, composed of two brigades, each of four independent infantry battalions supported by small units of auxiliary troops (mainly 'C' type units). The operational role of this type of division was centred primarily on counter-guerrilla duties in China and in the Philippines.

A Japanese division was commanded by a lieutenant-general, with a colonel serving as chief-of-staff. The staff was broken down into two sections: the general staff section and the administrative section. To the staff were attached five departmental sections, including intendance (supply), medical, veterinary, ordnance and judiciary. Also included were separate ordnance, veterinary, guard and signal detachments. In all, the strength of a division staff was approximately 300 officers and men. The general staff section comprised 75 officers and enlisted men, and was responsible for supply, communications, training (G-1), intelligence (G-2), rear services and supply (G-3), and adjutant. The administrative section was responsible for records maintenance, personnel and other administrative details.

The division's signal unit, commanded by a captain, consisted of two wire platoons, one radio platoon and a materials or equipment platoon, and numbered approximately 250 officers and enlisted men. Each wire platoon was divided into four sections of approximately 50 men each. The radio platoon was divided into sections each with one set, with strength varying from 8 to 12 men each. The approximate number of radios or wireless telephones was calculated to be around 32 telephones, 2 radio sets (ground-to-air), 48km (30 miles) of wire, and 8 to 10 other types of radios. The signal unit was equipped with pigeons, heliographs, semaphores and ground panels.

Above: Japanese tank crewmen discussing battle plans and tactics. The vehicle shown is a 1934 Model 89B Medium Tank. Unidentified armoured cars and another tank in the background suggest that they are taking part in large-scale manoeuvres.

The infantry group was led by a major-general. It consisted of a headquarters, an infantry group signal unit and three infantry regiments. In some instances, tankette companies with 80 to 120 men and 10 to 17 tankettes were assigned as support weapons for the infantry group. The infantry group's headquarters consisted of 70 to 100 officers and enlisted men. In the standard infantry division, a small signals unit was furnished, but the strengthened division had a fully fledged signals unit of 115 officers and men.

Some standard divisions had a small tankette company organised into three or four platoons, with a company train and a total strength of 80 to 120 officers and enlisted men. Normally, the total tankette strength stood somewhere between 10 and 17 vehicles, and was used mainly for reconnaissance, transport or, in some instances, fire support.

The three infantry regiments of an infantry group were broken down into a regimental headquarters, a regimental signal company, a regimental infantry gun unit, a regimental anti-tank unit and three infantry battalions. The approximate strength of a Japanese regiment centred on 3843 officers and enlisted men. The regimental headquarters comprised, in most cases, 55 officers and men. It consisted of a staff made up of administration, code, intelligence, ordnance and intendance sections. In addition to the latter sections, there was also an anti-aircraft section or headquarters guard. Total strength of the staff stood at 176 officers and

Below: A Japanese unit on bicycles in Che-kiang province, China, in June 1942. The Japanese used bicycles where possible to speed their movement across country, and by this means could outpace slower-moving Allied troops in the early part of the war.

enlisted men. Every regiment had a pioneer or labour unit of approximately 100 to 200 men which was composed of an officer, six sections and a materials section. There was also a regimental signal company of about 132 officers and men, consisting of a wire (line or L/T) platoon and one radio platoon. As for equipment, the signal company had anywhere from 12 to 20 telephone sets, 17.7km (11 miles) of insulated wire, 3 to 5 light radio sets, 2 or 3 ground radio sets, ground-to-air panels, dog sections, pigeons and heliograph and other equipment sections.

The Rifle Regiment

Every regiment had an infantry gun company consisting of a headquarters element, two platoons (of four guns) and an ammunition platoon. Total strength of the gun company was 122 officers and enlisted men. The armament of the regimental gun company consisted of two regimental guns and two anti-tank guns, instead of the standard four 75mm (2.95in) regimental infantry guns. Sometimes, the Japanese substituted 81mm (3.2in) mortars in lieu of the standard field guns. Supplementing the firepower of the infantry regiment was a regimental gun battalion that consisted of a small headquarters staff and two 'Type A' 75mm gun companies. Each company was assigned four guns and an ammunition platoon. There was a regimental anti-tank company that consisted of a headquarters detachment and a firing unit of three platoons to deal with enemy tanks. Each platoon came equipped with two anti-tank guns, making for a total of six per company. During the course of the war, as the Japanese Army came across overwhelming Allied armour superiority, they added a company of 130

officers and men and increased the number of guns to four per company in the strengthened infantry division.

The Rifle Battalion

The standard Japanese Army infantry battalion, commanded by a major, consisted of a headquarters, a train, four rifle companies, a machine-gun company and a battalion gun platoon. Its wartime fighting strength was 1100 officers and men with 677 rifles, 36 grenade launchers, 37 light machine guns, 12 heavy machine guns (7.7mm (0.31in)), and 2 battalion guns (70mm (2.75in)).

The strengthened infantry battalion consisted of 1626 officers and enlisted men, made up of a headquarters staff, four rifle companies, a machine-gun company, a battalion gun company and a battalion anti-tank company. It was broken down into 730 rifles, 37 light machine guns, 49 grenade launchers, 4 heavy machine guns (7.7mm), 8 20mm anti-tank rifles, 4 37mm anti-tank guns, and 4 battalion guns (70mm).

The strengthened (modified) infantry battalion consisted of a headquarters staff, a train, four rifle companies, a machine-gun company and a battalion gun company. It stood at about 1401 enlisted men, 750 rifles, 37 light machine guns, 49 grenade dischargers, 12 heavy machine guns (7.7mm), 8 anti-tank rifles (20mm) and 4 battalion guns (70mm).

Below: A Japanese machine gun unit moves cautiously forward past two abandoned Russian armoured cars while fighting the Soviet Red Army along the Mongolian border in July 1939. Note the wooden poles for carrying the machine gun in one swift move.

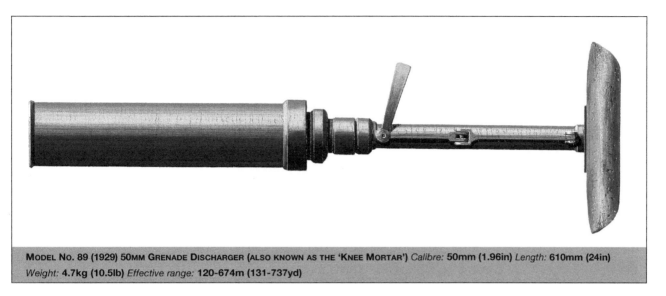

MODEL No. 89 (1929) 50MM GRENADE DISCHARGER (ALSO KNOWN AS THE 'KNEE MORTAR') *Calibre:* **50mm (1.96in)** *Length:* **610mm (24in)** *Weight:* **4.7kg (10.5lb)** *Effective range:* **120-674m (131-737yd)**

The most obvious difference in the three types of battalions found in any Japanese infantry division was the twofold increase in rifle and heavy guns which increased the firepower available to a Japanese Army commander.

The Rifle Company

The Infantry Rifle Company 'B' Type consisted of a company commander, normally a captain, a company headquarters and three rifle platoons. The total wartime strength of this type of infantry company was 181 officers and enlisted men. Each infantry company type 'B' had 139 rifles, 9 light machine guns and 9 grenade dischargers. The Infantry Rifle Company 'A' Type consisted of a company commander, company headquarters and three rifle platoons. Total strength was 205 officers and enlisted men. There were 150 rifles, 9 light machine guns and 12 grenade dischargers. The Infantry Rifle Company 'A' type with heavy weapons – the standard infantry company during the war – consisted of the same units as both the 'B' and 'without heavy weapons' types, but had an additional ammunition platoon attached, bringing its strength to 262 officers and enlisted men. Its weaponry stood at 150 rifles, 9 light machine guns, 12 grenade launchers, 2 heavy machine guns and 2 anti-tank guns (20mm (0.79in)).

Support Weapons

The lessons learned from the Western Front during World War I emphasised the importance of machine guns as a means of fire support during an infantry assault. Here, the Japanese Army organised both an eight- and a four-gun machine-gun company in order to meet any tactical situation The standard eight-gun battalion machine-gun company consisted of a headquarters, a firing unit of four platoons (each having two heavy 7.7mm machine guns) and an ammunition platoon. The total strength of this machine-gun company was 144 officers and enlisted men; it was the most common machine-gun company Allied forces encountered in the South and Central Pacific during World War II. The other machine-gun company type found at battalion level was the four-gun company, which had four guns assigned to it. The other six were normally detailed to accompany rifle companies and appeared in the strength of that particular rifle company. This type of machine-gun company consisted of a headquarters, two gun platoons and a small ammunition platoon.

The battalion gun platoon comprised a headquarters, a firing unit of two gun sections of one 70mm gun each, and an ammunition section. Its total strength was 55 officers and enlisted men. There was also a battalion-level gun company – minus the anti-tank rifles – with the normal organisation, except with two platoons and an ammunition platoon. Its strength was around 122 officers and enlisted men and four 70mm guns. The battalion gun company with anti-tank rifles had a firing unit of two gun platoons with 70mm howitzers, four platoons of 20mm anti-tank guns, and an ammunition platoon. Total strength was around 230 officers and men.

Among the independent infantry formations were the independent infantry group, infantry brigade, mixed brigade and amphibious brigades. The independent infantry groups had three infantry regiments without supporting arms or combat support and combat service support units. The independent infantry brigades consisted of four infantry battalions and a signal unit; estimated strength was 4900 officers and men. The independent mixed brigades were formed primarily as counter-guerrilla units

Above: Japanese tanks and tankettes enter a village in China during World War II. Their Chinese opponents lacked both armour and anti-tank artillery, so even relatively small armoured units could dominate the battlefield.

and were found primarily in China. The total strength of these units, which the Japanese High Command eventually transformed into standard infantry divisions, stood at around 6000 to 10,000 men. These were considered to be 'shock' units and, as such, had tanks, anti-aircraft guns and medium artillery attached. The infantry element consisted of three regiments of four companies each. One brigade was reported to be completely motorised.

Perhaps the most interesting formations were the amphibious brigades. These units comprised a headquarters and three battalions with a strength of about 3200 officers and men. The rifle companies of the amphibious brigades were made up of three platoons of five sections each, a trench mortar platoon, and a heavy weapons platoon. The trench mortar company consisted of three platoons of four sections each, while the gun company had three mountain- and two anti-tank guns. The 1st Amphibious Brigade had supporting artillery, tank, engineer, machine cannon and signal units directly under a brigade headquarters. Total personnel for this unit stood at 4000 and was led by a major-general.

Other infantry formations included independent infantry regiments and battalions, infantry mortar units (*Hakugeki tai*) and artillery mortar units (*Kyuho tai*). Tank groups in the Japanese Army – of three to four regiments, plus a signals unit – each had 250 tanks, 8 105mm (4.1in) and 4 155mm (6.1in) howitzers, and attached anti-aircraft guns, machine guns, engineer, transport and medical units.

There was also an independent tank regiment – made up of three or four companies and a regimental ammunition train – which had a strength of between 800 and 850 men, and some 85 to 95 light or medium tanks. There were reports that variants of this regiment existed, consising of a headquarters, 1 light tank company (10 light tanks), 2 medium tank companies (each with 10 medium tanks and 2 light tanks) and a regimental train. Total strength was estimated to be around 700 officers and enlisted men, with approximately 60 tanks of all types.

There was also a cavalry brigade tank unit which consisted of a headquarters, two companies of light tanks and a unit train. The companies, of 3 platoons each, included 10 light tanks and a company ammunition train. Total personnel unit strength was 350 officers and enlisted men with 30 tanks and 80 trucks. There were also independent tank companies, mixed brigade light- and medium tank units, and light armoured car or tankette companies.

The Infantry Division's Artillery Support

The standard field artillery component of a standard infantry division was a 36-gun regiment of 75mm field- or mountain guns, which was motorised, horse- and pack drawn. It consisted of a regimental headquarters, three battalions of 75mm guns and a regimental supply train. Total strength was about 2300 officers and men and normal armament was 36 75mm guns. Each of the three battalions consisted of a headquarters, three gun companies, and an artillery supply train. Artillery companies comprised a headquarters operational group, 2 gun platoons (each of 2 sections of 20 soldiers), and a supply train. The equipment found in an artillery battalion was 36 field guns, 450 rifles (roughly 138 per battalion and 34 per company) and approximately 2000 horses.

Organised along similar lines, a mountain artillery regiment had all the authorised equipment found in a standard artillery regiment, but also came armed with 36 75mm mountain guns. Its average strength was likewise larger. Personnel assigned to this type of artillery outfit numbered around 3000 to 3400 officers and enlisted men. Some mountain artillery regiments included a battalion of 105mm pack (mountain) howitzers.

There was also a mixed field artillery regiment, which consisted of a headquarters, a supply train and three battalions of 75mm field guns or 105mm howitzers. It numbered approximately 2380 officers and enlisted men and had a total of 12 75mm field guns and 24 105mm howitzers. There was also a medium artillery battalion of 950 officers and men, which had the normal headquarters components, as well as three companies of four 105mm howitzers. The artillery element in a strengthened infantry division consisted of an artillery group, comprising an artillery group headquarters and a field artillery regiment containing 75mm and 105mm howitzers. It also had a medium artillery battalion of 105mm howitzers.

Standard Japanese artillery units included field units, mountain units, medium units and heavy artillery units. The latter included 240mm (9.4in) howitzers, 300mm (11.9in) mortars and 150mm (5.9in) howitzers. Medium Japanese artillery included Type '96 150mm field howitzers and 105mm howitzers. Light artillery units had both 75mm and 105mm howitzers, and 81mm mortars. Their organisation was similar to that of the field artillery regiment or battalion which was found in an infantry division, with

the exception that the regiments had a total of only two – instead of the standard number of three – battalions.

Other Support Units

Each standard and strengthened infantry division had a cavalry and a reconnaissance regiment or unit. Each cavalry regiment comprised a headquarters squadron and supply train, three rifle or sabre companies and a mounted machine-gun company. Total strength was 950 officers and men. The reconnaissance regiment comprised a divisional cavalry troop, used as an alternative to a cavalry regiment. A standard reconnaissance regiment comprised a headquarters, one cavalry company, two motorised companies, one armoured car or light tankette company, and one motor truck company. Total strength was 730 officers and men.

As for the tank units present in all US Marine and US Army divisions during World War II, only the strengthened divisions had an organic tank unit equipped with light- and medium tanks. Most Japanese divisions maintained tankettes or light tanks. These tank units were found in group tankette companies or in reconnaissance regiments. US troops reported that the Japanese division tank units had about 20 light- and 48 medium tanks, some of which were held in reserve within the combat train. Tank units consisted of a headquarters unit, one light tank company, two medium tank companies and a combat field train. About 80 motor trucks or lorries were included in the supply train.

There were also a number of independent anti-tank battalions and companies, as well as cavalry brigade anti-tank units. Anti-aircraft units, especially machine-gun

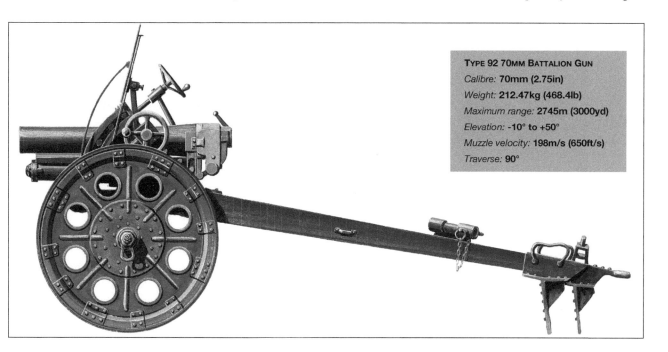

TYPE 92 70MM BATTALION GUN
Calibre: **70mm (2.75in)**
Weight: **212.47kg (468.4lb)**
Maximum range: **2745m (3000yd)**
Elevation: **-10° to +50°**
Muzzle velocity: **198m/s (650ft/s)**
Traverse: **90°**

Above: In northern Burma during World War II, Japanese engineers were forced to repair railway bridges damaged by the British as they retreated. Engineer companies were called upon to repair the bridges as fast as possible to maintain the pace of the advance.

cannon companies, were designed to fulfil a dual anti-aircraft/anti-tank role in an emergency.

Every standard and strengthened division had a three-company engineer regiment – comprising a headquarters, three companies of four platoons, and a regimental materials platoon – with an average strength of approximately 900 to 1000 officers and men. The average strength of an engineer company was 250 officers and men.

Japanese combat engineers were trained in digging tank traps, demolition work and small river-crossing operations. All companies within the engineer unit were trained to carry out all the different functions required by an infantry company or battalion. There was no specialisation among Japanese engineer companies organic to the Japanese infantry division, but there were specialised units, such as bridging and pontoon, for expert engineering work. Independent and mixed engineer companies and battalions were tactically organised along similar standard lines.

As for medical support, every Japanese infantry division had an extensive medical service organic to its composition.

Above: Japanese wounded rest in a field hospital at Tokuna Shima, Okinawa. The medical ward is dug into a hillside to protect it from shelling or bombing by American forces. Each Japanese division had its own medical service responsible for its troops.

Medical units in the Japanese Army included a medical unit, three to five field hospitals, and a water purification unit. In addition, other components of the division included a number of medically trained personnel. Clearly, Japanese Army officials wanted to facilitate the quick return of their wounded to their fighting units. Also, contrary to the rules established by the Geneva Convention and the Red Cross, Japanese medical personnel were reportedly armed and often fought as infantrymen.

Medical units in the Japanese Infantry Division consisted of a headquarters and supply train, three collecting companies of three stretcher platoons, and one ambulance platoon each. Personnel strength numbered approximately 700 to 1000 officers and enlisted men. The collecting companies each had about 20 litters and 15 ambulances. Headquarters trains had additional carts for loading medical supplies, patients' clothing and chemical warfare decontamination material. Other medical personnel were likewise assigned to infantry battalions. Battalion medical officers were usually assigned two NCO assistants. Each company had medical orderlies to dress wounds and administer basic first aid.

Other support units included transport, veterinary, ordnance, chemical warfare and water purification. Only the strongest divisions had chemical warfare troops; these men were motorised or horse-drawn. The chemical warfare detachment had a smoke unit which laid smokescreens.

SPECIALISED UNITS

Like the Allies during World War II, the Japanese created special units for special operational or tactical missions. Perhaps the most important were the parachute forces and naval infantry (*Rikusentai*) units created prior to the war.

The parachute battalion was made up of a battalion headquarters and three rifle companies of three platoons each. Each platoon had two rifle sections – each of six riflemen and an anti-tank group – and one heavy weapons section with a heavy machine-gun section of nine men and a cannon section of five men. The total strength of a parachute battalion was 600 to 700 officers and men.

In amphibious warfare, 'Japan entered World War II as well prepared as the United States, both in terms of operational forces and published doctrine.' In fact, the Japanese Navy and Army used their interventions in China as a testing ground for their amphibious warfare doctrine. As a result, the Japanese High Command was able to make major adjustments to their amphibious warfare doctrine and force structure. While its army took the

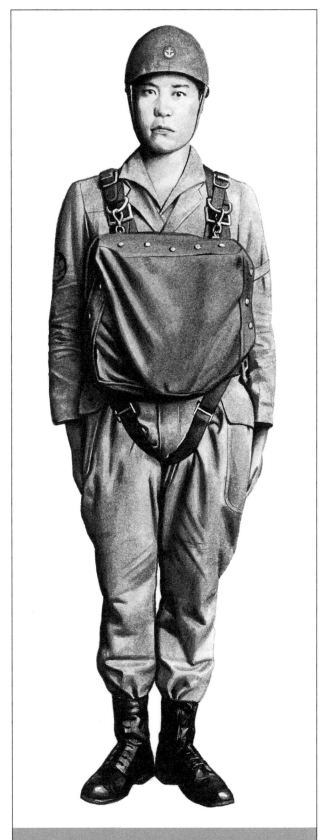

A Japanese paratrooper in field uniform and jump suit. He wears special boots to support his ankles when landing.

lead in the development of ampbhibious warfare doctrine during the early- to mid-1920s, its Navy concentrated on the development of small, highly mobile and lightly-armed naval infantry regiments. The latter were adequate for the capture of the weakly defended US-controlled islands in the Pacific such as Wake, Midway and Guam.

In fact, Japan had two forces capable of carrying out amphibious operations: the first force was the Army, which trained to conduct amphibious operations with a division or above; the second force, the Navy, was capable of carrying out regimental to platoon-level landing operations. While the Army maintained its forces according to current tables of organisation in order to conduct land operations once ashore, the Navy created several different organisational structures to deal with specific operational requirements, such as seizure or defence.

The Japanese first organised the special naval landing forces, or *Rikusentai*, in the late 1920s; they were often referred to as Japanese marines. While the *Rikusentai* did have a naval background, they were more of an island

---

Below: Japanese paratroopers board a waiting transport before carrying out a training jump before the war. The Japanese army was one of the first to set up specialist paratroop units, although they did not see service in the Pacific theatre.

defence force than an amphibious assault force. These naval infantry units, formed at the four major Japanese naval bases of Sasebo, Kure, Maizuru and Yokosuka, were given numerical designations.

The *Rikusentai* were composed entirely of naval personnel with a naval officer, usually a commander, in command. They were first used extensively in the many landing operations conducted along the China coast in 1932 and often undertook garrison duty upon capturing their objectives. While foreign observers noted that the *Rikusentai*'s performance was excellent when unopposed, this seemed not to be the case when they met determined opposition. One US Marine observer in China noted: 'they exhibited a surprising lack of ability in infantry combat'. In fact, while these naval infantry forces demonstrated that they could carry out amphibious operations, they also brought to the fore the inherent weaknesses of the *Rikusentai*, weaknesses which the Allied forces exploited from 1942 onwards.

These early special naval landing forces were organised as battalions, estimated to be about 2000 officers and men, divided into 4 companies. Three companies had six rifle platoons and one heavy machine-gun platoon; the fourth consisted of three platoons of four 76mm (3in) naval guns or two 75mm regimental guns and two 70mm battalion guns. Tanks and armoured car units were employed in

Above: Japanese *'Rikusentai'* or Marines haul their boats onto the beaches of Saipan during the Pacific War. Unlike their American counterparts, they use traditional wooden craft to make their way to the shore.

with an additional rifle company thereby increasing the firepower of the *Rikusentai*. By November 1943, the additional rifle company included 3 platoons of 1 officer and 48 enlisted men each (3 light machine-gun squads and 1 grenade discharge squad) and a heavy machine-gun platoon of 1 officer, 58 enlisted men and 8 heavy machine guns.

This was the same type of force that engaged the US Marines at Tarawa in the Gilberts and in the Marshalls in early 1944. The total operrational strength of the modified Type 1944 *Rikusentai* was 1820 officers and enlisted men.

In the *Rikusentai* it was the platoon, and not the company, which was the basic tactical unit. While it followed the same tactical doctrine as the Army, and its training – particularly for infantry – closely resembled that of the Army, prior to World War II it also received extensive training in landing operations and beach defences. However, one US Army observer noted: 'their training does not appear to have been up to the standard of the Japanese Army'. As their mission changed from offensive to defensive warfare, the Japanese Navy placed greater emphasis on infantry training for its existing marine units.

garrison duty and, where the terrain and situation favoured their use, in assault landing operations.

At the commencement of World War II in the Pacific, the special naval landing forces first seized then garrisoned the many island atolls conquered by the Japanese Army and naval forces. Both Wake Island and Tarawa in the Gilbert Islands were garrisoned solely by special landing forces. Reflecting the flexibility in Japanese force structure at the time, these naval landing forces were built around two rifle companies, each one in possession of a machine gun platoon and two companies of heavy weapons (anti-tank, anti-aircraft or tanks). Strength of these mobile units stood at about 1200 to 1500 men.

When Japan's armed forces went over to the defensive, so too did the *Rikusentai*. They now assumed a greater role in manning fixed defensive positions – which included fixed mounted naval guns – throughout the Central Pacific. Also, as a result of this change of mission, so too did the special naval landing force's organisation. The Japanese Navy and Army officials reinforced this

Below: *Rikusentai* disembark from a landing craft during the assault on Borneo in December 1941. A criticism of the *Rikusentai* was that they performed less well when making an opposed landing on a beach against a determined defence.

CHAPTER 4

Offensive and Defensive Tactics, 1931–1945

Although the war fought in the Pacific from 1941 onwards was very different from that fought in China, Japanese soldiers proved quick to adapt to the jungle and were able to exploit the terrain against the Allies. When the war turned against them, however, the Japanese became defensive experts.

SINCE THE END OF WORLD WAR II, the Japanese Army has often been depicted as a force incapable of launching anything but frontal assaults. While this characterisation has some truth, it nonetheless ignores the fact that the Japanese Army, during both the interwar era and World War II, proved to be innovative, flexible and highly effective on the modern battlefield. Indeed, the image of the wartime Japanese soldier clad in a torn uniform adorned with camouflage has become etched in most minds from studies of the fighting that took place in Burma, the Solomon Islands and New Guinea. What is usually forgotten is that, during the 1920s, the Japanese Army mainly prepared to fight not the United States Army, but rather the Soviet Army.

The Japanese Army of World War II was a tactically flexible and proficient fighting force built primarily along European lines. Japanese soldiers fought against regular military forces of the Western powers, most notably those of the United States and Great Britain, and the Soviet Union, as well as against guerrilla armies such as the Chinese nationalists and communists in China and Filipino guerrillas in the Philippines. They fought on the frozen steppes of Mongolia against the Soviet Army led by

Marshal Georgi Zhukov; in the hills and valleys of China and Manchuria against the nationalist forces of Generalissimo Chiang Kai-shek and the communists under Mao Zedong; in the steaming jungles of Burma against British, Indian and US forces; and against US Marines and soldiers on the many atolls and islands of the South and Central Pacific oceans. In fact, much of the success of the Japanese Army was not due to its ability to fight in the jungle, but rather to the fact that its tactical flexibility permitted it to operate on terrain suitable to the application of modern warfare principles of open and mechanised warfare. This flexibility was no accident, as prior to its introduction into a geographic area, the army was organised, trained and equipped in various operational and tactical techniques designed in each case to fit the terrain and meet the logistical requirements peculiar to the Japanese Army itself.

OFFENSIVE OPERATIONS, 1931–1943

As adherents to the code of *Bushido*, the Japanese unsurprisingly placed great emphasis on offensive operations, the element of surprise, and rapid deployment. Japanese military doctrine was based on 'the principle that a single plan, carried through with power and determination, coupled with speed and maneuver, will so disrupt the plans of hostile forces that success will ensue'. In order to ensure this rapid movement and determination,

Left: This dramatic photograph shows the Japanese marines in action in 1932, storming the Chinese city of Shanghai. The tactics and equipment used by the Japanese in World War II were refined during their interventions in China in the 1930s.

Japanese commanders and staffs operated well forward of their forces in order to keep themselves informed of the situation as it developed on the battlefield. In every combat order issued on the battlefield, these officers and staffs stressed that 'the enemy will be annihilated'. While the Japanese Army emphasised the need to achieve surprise whenever and wherever possible, it was envelopment that was the 'preferred' method of attack. Japanese soldiers also became practitioners of thorough reconnaissance and the infiltration of enemy positions throughout World War II.

Finally, much of the Japanese Army's tactical doctrine was based on *Bushido* and the idea that the Japanese soldier's ability was 'far superior' to that of his enemies. This sense of military superiority – based on 'face' and 'toughness' – contributed to the Japanese soldier's willingness to attack a well-defended position in spite of little or no chance of success on many occasions throughout World War II.

Flaws in Japanese tactical doctrine did, however, exist. No sense of 'military superiority' could overcome the numerical, technological and operational capabilities of its opponents during the war. In fact, what failed the Japanese Army during World War II was that much of its doctrine had been based on its experiences against the Russians and Chinese during the 1930s. The tactical doctrine and

methods employed by the Japanese Army during World War II were those considered appropriate for fighting in open country such as North Asia. In fact, it is here that one can see the similarities in methods between the French and German armies in Japanese tactical doctrine, as the latter were quick to copy and possibly 'improve' on the tactics of their enemies. This was seen in the latter stages of World War II when, instead of attempting to stop an amphibious landing at the beachhead, Japanese Army doctrine emphasised that the landing was to go ahead largely unopposed until such time that sufficient firepower could be brought against the advancing enemy forces. This tactic was learned and passed on to the Japanese by their German allies after the D-Day landings at Normandy on 6 June 1944. It was employed against the US Marines and Army from Peleliu in September 1944 through to Iwo Jima in February 1945, and later during the Okinawa campaign in April 1945. Frequently, the local commander would dictate the type of tactics to be employed against the landing.

Much like the French Army's pre-World War I regulations, Japanese tactical doctrine emphasised the offensive, a fact repeatedly stressed in that army's Field Service Regulations in the 1920s and 1930s. Like that of the US Marine Corps and Army during World War II, the 'object of offensive operations was to 'maneuver and close quickly with the enemy'. This was to ensure that the perceived Japanese superiority in close combat could be employed. Indeed, the defensive was considered only to be a transitory phase and the Japanese commander

Below: Japanese troops move forward against the Chinese in Manchuria with the support of a machine gun post. Note their cold weather uniforms – a world away from the conditions encountered in the Pacific.

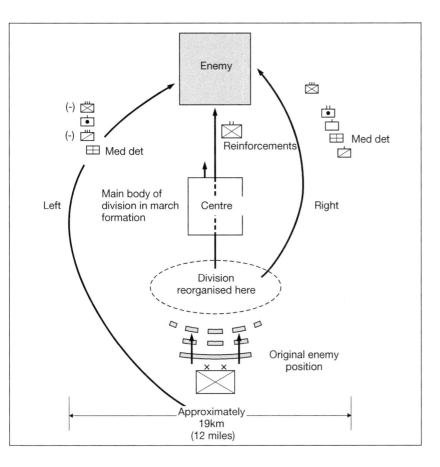

Left

Med det

Reinforcements

Med det

Main body of
division in march
formation

Centre

Right

Enemy

Division
reorganised here

Original enemy
position

Approximately
19km
(12 miles)

Above: A diagram showing how a Japanese division would break through and envelop an enemy position before launching an enveloping pursuit. These tactics were used to great effect by the Japanese during their advance in the early part of the war.

where, by all orthodox tactics, the situation patently required some form of defensive action'. This had the inevitable results of many casualties and a failure to achieve the objective. Use of such tactics likewise led to the inability of Japanese commanders to concentrate all of their forces at hand and effectively employ combined arms during an attack.

OFFENSIVE OPERATIONS

By far, Japanese Army commanders considered the envelopment as the preferred offensive manoeuvre. The use of envelopment tactics was inevitably accompanied by a determined frontal assault, while the main force attacked an exposed enemy flank. An envelopment could be a single, double or a complete encirclement known as *kanzen hoi*. Japanese commanders preferred to launch double envelopments, so as to ensure maximum surprise and shock effect. This was often carried out by an insufficient number of troops forced to rely more heavily on surprise and deception. Based on the manpower available, a Japanese commanders sought to envelop an enemy force through one of several methods.

was to use 'every effort to regain the offensive and take the initiative'. Even while on the defence, offensive principles were strongly emphasised. The inculcation of this training and faith in offensive operations often led individual Japanese commanders to 'reach attack decisions

The units in the division which were executing the frontal holding attack while the other elements manoeuvred around the enemy's flanks often made a close-in envelopment when executing this move. Units of this frontal holding attack, normally squads and platoons, always sought to utilise the

JAPANESE ARMY ENVELOPMENT TACTICS

Tactics	Unit Employed
a. The force advances in two or more parallel columns directed towards an enemy flank and rear during the advance to contact.	Division-sized unit
b. The force advances with certain units in the rear which can later be deployed to execute a flank movement.	Regiment, battalion, company and platoon
c. After the force has encountered the enemy and partially deployed, some units may be moved laterally for envelopment, if natural cover, darkness, fog or smoke are present.	Division and below

Left: A Japanese squad clear a narrow lane in Malaya in January 1942. The Japanese developed this technique while fighting the British. The submachine gunner and two riflemen cover their comrade as he cautiously checks the passage for the enemy.

effects of what the Japanese called *shageki hoi* (flanking fire). Given the emphasis they placed in peacetime training on terrain sketching and reconnaissance, Japanese commanders always took into consideration the terrain they would have to manoeuvre over, as well as likely avenues of approach of an enemy's reserves and heavy weapons.

In order to achieve the maximum amount of surprise and shock during the envelopment, Japanese commanders often sent a small force, usually a platoon or squad, around to attack the enemy in his rear areas. When this manoeuvre, called a *ukai*, was used, the force sent around to the enemy's rear was normally a battalion which had been reinforced by light artillery and a squad of combat engineers. The mission of such a turning force was often similar to that of a pursuit detachment. If the *ukai* was

Below: Troops advancing on the Chinese city of Hankau in 1938 hold their position while they observe the results of a Japanese artillery bombardment on the enemy's positions. Against stronger opponents such a prominent display of a flag would be suicidal.

successful, the 'turning force' became a pursuit force if the main assault also succeeded.

According to Japanese Army regulations, frontal attacks were discouraged. Nevertheless, during World War II, Japanese commanders made frequent use of frontal assaults in order to disrupt the enemy's ability to reinforce or consolidate his defensive positions. In fact, this type of attack occurred quite frequently on Guadalcanal and throughout the Northern Solomons campaigns. As expected, a frontal assault was normally launched against a supposed weak spot in the enemy's defences. Marine Sergeant George MacGilivrary recalled that the Japanese used this type of assault with some success on Guadalcanal in late October 1942. After conducting probing attacks against various points in the line, the main assault would follow, aimed at breaching the enemy's main lines with the goal of penetrating swiftly and deeply to his rear area. The Japanese attempted this manoeuvre on Guadalcanal throughout October 1942, with the objective of seizing Henderson Airfield. Even as the frontal assault took place, the Japanese commander sought to maintain a narrow battle front with the units involved. Dispositions were made in depth and coordinated with artillery. Tanks, if

Above: Japanese and Indian soldiers occupy a trench in Burma, 1944. A number of pro-independence Indians joined the Japanese-organised Indian National Army to fight against the British. The Japanese also recruited Koreans and Formosans into their army.

available, were used in order to exploit the situation. While the Japanese Army in general was weak in overall use of artillery support during the war, its attacking infantry depended heavily on the portable mortars and infantry assigned to the infantry battalion to provide fire support.

Positive Action

In short, the Japanese attacked during World War II when the 'orthodox' or accepted decision had called for less positive action. The use of the frontal assault – often mistaken by the enemy for the *banzai* attack – while both costly in terms of manpower and considered to be hasty in terms of execution, nonetheless was never found to be lacking in vigour and determination. Furthermore, it is important to emphasise that Japanese troops often conducted a frontal assault without proper coordination of combined arms and, in some instances, without any assistance from Japanese supporting arms.

Above: Japanese assault troops disembark from inflatable dinghys on a river in the Malay Penisula during the offensive against the British in January 1942. Rivers provided a swift and relatively easy way to move troops forward during the Japanese advance.

war: bold, decisive and swift action. According to one Japanese military commentator: 'The Imperial Army seeks to wage a short war to a quick and decisive conclusion. The meeting engagement conforms to this spirit and is to be sought whenever possible.'

One last aspect concerning the meeting engagement involved the movement to contact. Here, the Japanese Army preferred the use of parallel columns, each self-contained, and proceeded in formation by an advanced guard with the heavy use of motorised infantry as a reconnaissance force to scout and occupy a desired terrain feature. If a meeting engagement became likely while on the march, the division commander modified the formation en route to contact and prepared his force to envelop either one or both flanks of the enemy. This move contained the 'germ' of the manouevre which the division commander expected to adopt if he encountered the enemy on the march, especially as strong advance guards were characteristic of the Japanese Army as it approached a meeting engagement.

By far the most heavily employed and most favoured tactic of the Japanese Army was the meeting engagement. In fact, 'the meeting engagement was the foundation of Japanese combat training, with official regulations giving more space to it than any other form of combat'. Japanese manuals stressed that 'the meeting engagement was the collision of two hostile forces in motion, or the meeting of a force in motion with one which has halted but has not had time to organize a detailed position'. With this in mind, the Japanese Army strongly emphasised the meeting engagement when training its soldiers for combat. This tactic, in fact, followed the Japanese desire for swift and decisive offensive action.

In the meeting engagement, Japanese Army manuals stressed that there were four basic rules that governed the use of this tactic in battle: (i) the seizure and retention of the initiative; (ii) bold, independent action by subordinate commanders; (iii) prompt occupation of important terrain features; and (iv) energetic leadership during combat. What was even more important was the fact that the meeting engagement conformed closely to the Japanese way of

Extensive Reconnaissance

On the march to the meeting engagement, a Japanese Army commander would carry out an extensive reconnaissance of the enemy, terrain and time and place, in order to determine where he might seek battle. After all this information was collated, a Japanese commander issued a fragmentary operational order so as to initiate the deployment of the division. Japanese Army Combat Regulations warned commanders against waiting for overly detailed information before deciding to attack.

While Japanese commanders preferred to conduct a coordinated attack against an enemy's main forces, they often resorted to hasty, piecemeal attacks. The coordinated attack usually followed the meeting engagement, whereby columns deployed directly behind the so-called 'line of departure', or the initial point of the attack. As for the piecemeal attack, Japanese commanders normally committed their troops upon arrival at the objective. This commonly resulted in units being either cut off or annihilated due to the hasty, decentralised command and control that accompanied such a manoeuvre. Units in the

AVERAGE FRONTAGES DURING A JAPANESE ARMY ATTACK	
Company	206m (225 yds)
Battalion	366–549m (400–600yds)
Regiment	1006m (1100yds)

assault likewise lost their alignment with the main body when conducting a piecemeal attack. Throughout World War II, Japanese commanders displayed an 'excessive willingness' to use the piecemeal attack.

As for the assault, while the attacking infantry approached the enemy's positions, both infantry and artillery fire was increased and reserve units were brought up. These reserve units were used to extend and exploit any advantage gained in the main assault, to meet a counter-attack, or to extend the flank of the enveloping forces.

As for the meeting engagement itself, witness reports indicated that the Japanese carried them out with boldness and vigour. As the regulations stipulated, speed in both

decision and execution were the usual hallmarks of these types of attacks.

Despite the inherent faults in the desire to engage rapidly in the attack upon reaching an objective, Japanese commanders adhered to seven basic principles that they carried out in all theatres of operation throughout World War II. These were: (1) rapid, aggressive offensive action by all elements; (2) a tendency to carry out uncoordinated piecemeal actions; (3) development behind weakly linked covering forces; (4) frontal attack or restricted close-in developments; (5) inadequate artillery support; (6) sacrifice of proper reconnaissance and organisation to obtain speed in attack; and (7) conducting attacks through terrain generally considered to be impossible or impenetrable.

As the fighting throughout the island chains in the Pacific Ocean area intensified, Japanese commanders many times sought to overcome enemy positions by launching

Below: A Japanese Type 89 tank advances over a destroyed bridge in China in 1937, accompanied by an infantry section. Other soldiers wait on the bank to see if the structure will support the tank's weight.

Above: Japanese troops advance along a Malayan river as they approach Singapore from the north. Japanese soldiers in Malaya became skilled jungle fighters, and this gave them the advantage when attacking British forces.

displace and whether or not time was of the essence. When the continuous attack was made, the attacking infantry usually paused briefly on the captured position before continuing the attack. As for the actual technique of attack, the typical disposition of the infantry in the assault was into wings, with the preponderance of strength in one wing assigned to make the main effort, while the other wing made the secondary attack. In accordance with their deployment, infantry units advanced from the assembly area to assigned positions along the line of departure, where final attack preparations were made. The hour of attack was usually assigned to about one to two hours after dawn. Under normal conditions, the Japanese commanders had a preference for launching assaults before dawn, although they were just as capable of launching a night attack. Japanese commanders remained hesitant to launch such attacks in the dark, however, because of problems with adjusting their artillery. When the Japanese Army launched attacks in the daylight, it normally required at least four hours between the attack order being issued and the actual assault taking place.

continuous, sustained attacks, normally in two phases over a 24-hour period. Attacks were launched against both the enemy's outpost and main positions. The decision to launch a continuous attack, however, was based on the availability of artillery support without the latter having to

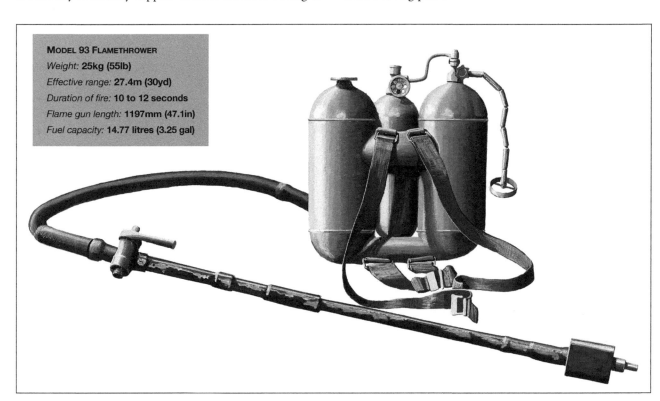

MODEL 93 FLAMETHROWER
Weight: **25kg (55lb)**
Effective range: **27.4m (30yd)**
Duration of fire: **10 to 12 seconds**
Flame gun length: **1197mm (47.1in)**
Fuel capacity: **14.77 litres (3.25 gal)**

PHASES, OBJECTIVES AND MISSION OF ARTILLERY SUPPORT IN THE ATTACK		
Phase	Objective	Mission
Phase I	Attack of the outpost position by two battalions, fire support to attacking infantry	Counterbattery by one battalion, direct support
Phase II	Occupation of outpost line to opening of artillery preparations	Counterbattery fire, harassing fire, interdiction fires
Phase III	Artillery preparation: duration of one to two hours	
Phase IV	Adjusting fires: 30 minutes in daylight; 30 minutes for wire-cutting, accompanied by slight counterbattery; half-fire on infantry positions	Direct support fires with particular attention to main effort

Japanese Army units also adhered to prescribed frontages during an attack. Frontages were 20 to 25 per cent greater for units making the secondary assault. As for the assembly of division reserves, this normally took place anywhere from 2.4km to 3.2km (1½ to 2 miles) from the line of departure.

When tanks were used in such attacks, Japanese Army commanders sought to achieve maximum surprise prior to their commitment to battle. At the position of attack, tanks were attached to frontline battalions and jumped off into the attack simultaneously with the infantry. The infantry were advised prior to the attack that if the tank either broke down or was destroyed, they were not to stop but were to continue the attack. Japanese commanders used tanks to destroy barbed wire and to destroy or neutralise enemy gun emplacements or fixed defences.

ARTILLERY SUPPORT IN THE ATTACK

When artillery was utilised, Japanese commanders normally received reinforcements in the way of both light- and medium artillery battalions. The Army's combat organisation provided for a direct support group of one or two battalions for each wing without artillery being used in general support. When a fourth battalion was attached, it usually acted in the counter-battery role. For fire missions, these roles normally differed, based on the phases of the proposed action.

All of the division artillery assets were utilised for an attack on an outpost line of resistance. Artillery positions were pushed forward to within 457–732m (500–800yd) of the infantry line of departure so that they could support the attack of the main position without moving. At the time of the attack on the main position, one or two artillery companies were often attached to the main effort as accompanying artillery. Ammunition allowances during an attack were estimated to be anywhere from three to three-and-a-half days allotment (whereby a day of a 75mm (2.95in) gun fire amounted to 300 rounds).

There was much criticism aimed at the effectiveness of Japanese artillery based on the fact that there simply was not enough of it. This came from a lack of appreciation of the effect of artillery in a direct-support role to an infantry attack. Furthermore, the Japanese Army concentrated the bulk of its artillery on lighter, more mobile field guns, with the inevitable result that it neglected its acquisition of much heavier field guns. The lack of adequate artillery and artillery fire in general reduced the flexibility at the disposal of a Japanese infantry commander when preparing for an assault. In fact, US Marine and US Army commanders were often surprised when Japanese attacks occurred with little or no artillery preparation or fire support. This lack of direct fire support often resulted in heavy casualties to the attacking force.

SUMMARY OF ATTACK OPERATIONS

This disregard for incurring heavy casualties can be seen in the fact that, no matter what the cost in lives, Japanese commanders were relentless in pressing an attack towards a successful conclusion. Their campaigns in the tropical countries of Malaya, Burma, Indonesia, Indochina, the Philippines and the Solomons did meet with great success during the first part of the war. This was due in large part, however, to the Japanese ability to adjust to the conditions of jungle warfare and capitalise on the handicaps of their adversaries' inability to adjust to similar conditions.

In relation to attack, therefore, the following observations can be made on the Japanese method of launching an assault. First, the Japanese employed careful, meticulous staff planning with detailed planning of the intended operation, the training and equipment necessary, and in the coordination and execution of the operation. Secondly, they showed boldness, both in the conception of the operation and in the carrying out of its details. Thirdly, there was a fearlessness of the enemy and the weapons he had at his disposal. Further, the Japanese showed a total disregard for casualties in attaining an objective. They also made extensive use of surprise and deception, and generally refrained from advancing to the attack before interdiction of all nearby enemy airfields and attainment of air superiority in the area of the attack. Finally, Japanese soldiers not only showed great speed in the infiltration, envelopment and pursuit of an enemy force, but also many Japanese commanders displayed a willingness to attack over terrain normally considered impassable and in all types of adverse weather conditions at any given time of day or night.

Japanese commanders conducted offensive operations along orthodox lines and, for the most part, with little or no deviation from combat regulations. Like most armies of the day, the Japanese Army by and large fought according to

the tactics it had developed in the 1920s during peacetime manoeuvres and later, during the 1930s, in combat operations in Manchuria and China. It applied these same tactics to the battlefields on Guadalcanal, throughout New Guinea and Burma, and on the island atolls of the Central Pacific. Despite this rigid orthodoxy, however, the Japanese soldier could adapt or improvise to any tactical situation.

PURSUIT OPERATIONS

Two last offensive-orientated tactics practised by the Japanese infantryman during World War II were the pursuit of a defeated enemy and conduct of night operations. In fact, Japanese regulations and tactical doctrine placed the normal emphasis on the need for pursuit of a defeated adversary in order to reap the full fruits of victory. Japanese commanders were strenuously urged to pursue the enemy relentlessly in order to avoid the consequent

Below: Japanese troops advance against British soldiers in Malaya, 1942. The frontal attack with bayonets was a common ploy used by the Japanese, but it could prove costly against a determined enemy.

need for another battle against a reorganised and possibly reinforced enemy.

Even while they conducted offensive operations, Japanese commanders planned for the pursuit. With this in mind, they normally kept a close eye on the situation on the battlefield, ready to exploit any sign of weakness on part of the enemy. To enhance their ability to know when to send reserves forwards and exploit the battlefield situation, Japanese commanders used reconnaissance either by cavalry or infantry forces, or by air plane. The Japanese categorised the pursuit into two types. The first type involved a scenario whereby an enemy was destroyed near the field of battle where he incurred his initial defeat. The second type of pursuit was where the enemy had partially succeeded in extricating his forces from the battle area. Here, the Japanese infantry had to continue the advance well into enemy territory. In both types of pursuit, the destruction of the enemy was accomplished by fixing him with direct pressure, while mobile pursuit detachments, moving around the flanks, occupied critical points along the enemy's line of retreat and fell upon his rear.

While both types of pursuit were practised during manoeuvres in the 1920s and 1930s, the Japanese Army

Above: A dramatic photograph of Japanese soldiers landing in Hong Kong. Speed and surprise gave the Japanese an advantage during their advance in the early part of the war, often catching Allied defences unawares.

preferred and extensively practised the second type of pursuit. Japanese Army commanders assumed that an enemy would break off contact before complete destruction ensued. Tactically, when a Japanese commander was made aware that an enemy was about to break contact, he then renewed the attack on his own initiative in an effort to push through or around the enemy's covering forces. As the Japanese units pushed through the enemy's positions, reserve units, formed into pursuit detachments, manoeuvred around the flanks of the objectives deep in the enemy's rear. When the Japanese frontline infantry passed through the area of resistance of the enemy's covering forces, the division commander temporarily halted them until reinforcements were sent in to continue the pursuit of the defeated enemy.

Tanks were used to block off an enemy's likely avenue of escape, as well as to attack his artillery batteries, command posts and communications centres. In order to avoid any

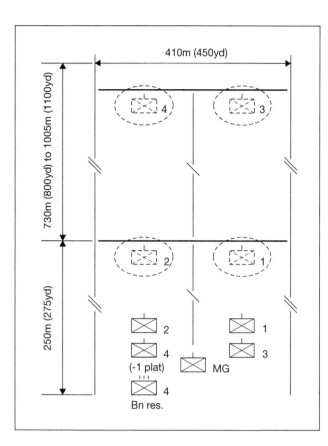

Above: A typical Japanese night attack formation. The Japanese were trained to operate at night and small units were prepared to advance independently of each other until contact was made with the enemy.

serious loss of control, the Japanese commander usually designated, prior to an attack, a phase line where the force was to converge, regroup and continue the pursuit. A part of the frontline infantry was then organised with previously formed pursuit detachments. The bulk of the division then re-formed and, in march columns, followed after the pursuit detachments.

Artillery was likewise used to disrupt, harass and also possibly to interdict and block an enemy's escape route. As the frontline troops penetrated into the covering force's positions, the artillery, attached to the infantry, followed close by in bounds behind the advancing troops. The artillery then concentrated its fire on the resisting enemy infantry. Some artillery was attached to pursuit detachments to give close support.

The Japanese used this type of pursuit to great effect against the forces of Generalissimo Chiang Kai-shek in North China. Here, the Japanese commanders were seen to take advantage of the extensive rail network to transport their pursuing troops, as well as the Japanese advantage in

kaisoku butai, or specialised motorised units, which gave rapidity to its pursuing units.

NIGHT OPERATIONS

Throughout World War II, the Japanese Army showed a strong partiality for carrying out night attacks. This form of combat favoured the use of the bayonet and was thus stressed throughout infantry training. Here, the Japanese had been encouraged in their faith in night attacks by successful experiences in the Russo–Japanese War and the subsequent operations in China during the early part of World War II. During that period, American commanders often referred to the Japanese use of the night attack as 'the specialty of the Japanese Army' and as a 'traditional' Japanese method.

Night attacks were considered appropriate for units that varied in size from company to divisions. Those situations that called for use of night operations included: (1) a large unit, normally a division, wishing to extend or complete a success during a daylight engagement into the night; (2) large units, normally a division, wanting to use a part of their forces to seize by surprise points needed to assist the attack by the following day; (3) using local night attacks to distract or mislead the enemy and conceal Japanese activity elsewhere, such as a night withdrawal or retrograde operation; (4) a large unit being deploying to prevent a hostile night withdrawal or to complete the defeat of the enemy before he could be reinforced; and (5) when superior enemy firepower prevented the reaching of an attack objective in daylight.

When the Japanese Army conducted a night attack, the infantry was formed into two assault echelons and one reserve formation. While the first assault echelon carried out the initial attack, the second echelon passed through the first echelon and attempted to seize the second objective. In general, a force of one or two platoons, commanded by an officer, was given the mission of attacking and occupying an enemy stronghold. A battalion generally attacked on a 411–503m (450–550yd) sector, with two rifle companies in the lead echelon, two companies less a platoon in the second wave and a platoon in battalion reserve. The battalion in the attack was expected to reach and occupy two objectives, the more distant one being some 1000m (1100yd) from the jump-off position. Where the rear objective was more distant than this, or the going more difficult, two battalions attacked in column, with the rear battalion being responsible for the taking of the second objective.

Night attacks were classified by the Japanese as *kishu* and *kyoshu*. *Kishu* is translated as 'attack by surprise', while *kyoshu* means 'attack by force'. The surprise attack was characterised by an infantry rush with bayonets, but without preparatory or accompanying fire by artillery or infantry weapons. Attack by force implied a coordinated accompanying fire and possibly an artillery preparation by artillery or mortars. The attack against the first objective during a night attack was an attack by surprise or *kishu*, unless the enemy was expecting a night attack; the attack of the second objective was an attack by force. During a night attack, a battalion of artillery was employed in support of an infantry regiment carrying out just such an attack. The artillery commander, after conferring with his counterpart in the infantry, prepared his artillery to support an on-call attack during night operations.

While night attacks against an enemy not determined to hold a position at all costs were successful, they proved to be very dangerous and, above all else, costly in terms of troops killed when up against an array of well-fortified and well-entrenched automatic weapons and field guns. This was proven during an attack against the US Marine 7th Regiment on Guadalcanal in late October 1942. Here, the Japanese launched a series of suicidal night attacks against the Marines' positions and were virtually annihilated by the leathernecks' withering .50 (12.7mm) calibre machine guns, mortar and 37mm (1.45in) anti-tank gun fire.

DEFENSIVE OPERATIONS

Defensive operations were normally frowned upon both officially and unofficially in the Japanese Army during World War II. In fact, the Japanese were reluctant to admit that they had been forced to engage in defensive operations. The official US Army manual on the Japanese Army stated: 'so pronounced was their dislike for the defensive that tactical problems illustrating this type of combat are extremely rare'. Nonetheless, after 1942, with the exceptions of Japanese field forces in Burma and China, the Japanese Army in general was thrown onto the defensive in order to meet the two-pronged offensive of Admiral Chester W. Nimitz's Central Pacific Drive and General Douglas MacArthur's South-west Pacific offensive, which had as its overall goal the liberation of the Philippines. The reluctance on the part of Japanese histories to admit that the Imperial Army engaged in this form of combat during World War II is understandable, given Japan's pronounced offensive doctrine as inscribed in the code of *Bushido*. Yet,

by 1943, with the exception of the Kwangtung Army in China, the Japanese Army (and Navy) was on the strategic and tactical defensive throughout the Pacific theatres of operations. Yet even here the Japanese proved resourceful as they inflicted on the Americans and other Allied troops such losses by firepower from well-fortified, man-made and natural defensive works that the initial disparity of forces became equalised, to the point that it allowed Japanese

A Leading Seaman from the *Rikusentai* carries a Type 96 light machine gun and a water bottle.

Above: An Australian in New Guinea checks a Japanese bunker for any remaining signs of life. One of the bunker's former occupants lies dead in the foreground. Sheets of corrugated tin were often used in Japanese bunker construction.

commanders to carry out limited offensive operations. This was especially the case on Iwo Jima (February–March 1945) and Okinawa (April–June 1945).

The object of the Japanese infantryman in the defence was to 'inflict on the superior enemy forces such losses by firepower, disposed appropriately on the terrain and behind man-made defensive works, that the initial disparity of forces becomes equalized to the point of authorizing a passage eventually to the offensive'. Doctrinally, the Japanese Army adhered to the Combat Regulations of 1938, known as *Sento Koyo*, and based solely on the discussion of defensive operations in the active defence, and the regulations known as the *Sakusen Yomurei* which were issued during the war as the tactical situation drastically altered. These took the passive defence, assumed mainly in the presence of overwhelming superior forces, as the typical case.

In the defence, the Japanese Army adhered to standard Western principles in the establishment of a defensible position. These included observation, protected flanks, fields of fire, covered lines of communications, and obstacles. As the Japanese Army was increasingly forced on the defensive by US, British, Australian and New Zealand forces, the Japanese emphasised the importance of anti-tank obstacles across the fronts and flanks of their positions. Japanese commanders maximised the use of cover and concealment in the defence, as well as the use of reconnaissance in order to best employ both artillery and mechanised assets.

Important Defensive Factors

In the selection, occupation and defence of a position, Japanese Army commanders took several factors into consideration when deciding on the establishment of a defensive position. These were: determination of the probable direction of the hostile attack; the probable direction of a division counter-attack or counter-offensive; anti-tank measures; the assignment of troops within the defensive area; the use of artillery including anti-aircraft; the composition and location of the division reserve; the use of tanks; communications and liaison; and supply.

As for organisation of the defensive position, the defence was always based on the main position, or *Shujinchitai*, and was held to the last man. Division commanders divided the defensive positions into right and left sectors (*chiku*), the defence of which was assigned to their two senior infantry commanders. In cases where the front was broad, such as a shoreline or plain, or where a counter-offensive was anticipated, Japanese commanders added a central sector. When such a defensive posture was assumed, the infantry forces were positioned along the main line of resistance by units of battalions, with the frontage determined by both the terrain and mission. When a broad defence was adopted, battalion centres of resistance were organised for all-round defence, whereby each interval or echelon of defence was covered by machine-gun and anti-tank fire. By using this method of deployment, reserve units, normally mobile ones, were kept as large as possible in order to exploit any weakening of the enemy's attack or to prevent a major breakthrough. Average defence frontages were from 740–1830m (800–2000yd), while in a broad defence, the average frontage along the main line of resistance was 2740m (3000yd).

Support and local reserve units were deployed behind the frontline infantry, in distances that ranged from a depth of 640m to 1370m (700–1500yd). Throughout the defensive zone, automatic weapons and anti-tank guns were echeloned in depth. Heavy machine guns were deployed along the support positions, from which they covered the front with interlocking fire. Mortars were usually bracketed in and around the defensive position to prevent a major enemy breakthrough.

The second type of defensive position was the outpost, or *Keikai Jinchi*, position. This type of position was garrisoned by troops dispatched by the sector commanders. The outpost line of resistance was generally 1370–2740m (1500–3000yd) in front of the main line of resistance, so as to be within supporting range of light artillery. Japanese combat regulations recommended the use of shorter distances in order that their troops could obtain the fire support provided by machine guns positioned along the main line of resistance.

The missions of the outpost line of resistance were: to obtain enemy information by observation and patrolling; to cover the main line of resistance and prevent its surprise; to delay the hostile attack on the main line of resistance; and to act as an advance defensive position (*Zenshin Jinchi*). Troops assigned to garrison the outpost line of resistance varied in strength according to the mission at hand. For the front of a division, one or two battalions of infantry were normal in the problems consulted in the combat regulations. Comments on these problems from captured documents indicate that the Japanese assigned an infantry company to every 1830m (2000yd) in an outpost line of resistance, with important points occupied with increased strength, while intervals were covered by observation and the fire of automatic weapons and mortars. In this context, the Japanese rarely ever organised in combat a continuous system of infantry and artillery fire in front of an outpost line of resistance.

Advanced Defensive Position

One last defensive position employed by the Japanese infantryman during World War II was the advanced defensive position, or *Zenshin Jinchi*. This was found in the area between the outpost line of resistance and the main battle position. The purposes of this defensive position were to prevent, for as long as possible, the occupation of critical points of terrain by hostile forces near the main

Right: A captured Japanese bunker built from logs and roughly camouflaged. The thickness of the bunker's roof demonstrates how difficult it was at times to destroy these positions with naval gunfire or air bombardment.

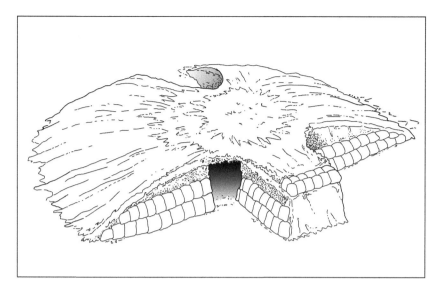

Above: Diagram of a Japanese bunker showing the entrance at the rear and the sandbags used in its construction. Japanese bunkers were never higher than an average soldier in height, and were placed to give a wide field of fire over the enemy.

were initially in forward positions in order to support the outpost positions or in an advanced defensive position. Japanese commanders normally echeloned artillery positions through a zone of about 2286m (2500yd) in depth that extended to the rear from a line which was of approximately 1555–2012m (1700–2200yd) behind the main line of resistance.

In those areas where the division commander elected not to organise an advanced position, the zone between the outpost position and the main battle position was covered by observers sent forwards by the frontline battalion commanders. These troops patrolled the foreground, cooperated with those posted on the outpost line of resistance and carried out local reconnaissance.

defensive zone; to delay the enemy preparations for the attack; and to induce the enemy to launch his attack in a false direction that would expose his flank. An advanced defensive position was typically used where, in order to obtain observation, the outpost line of resistance had been pushed well forwards, leaving an important ridge in the foreground of the main battle position ungarrisoned. It was also commonly used where an oblique line position was organised between the outpost position and the main battle position, with one flank resting on the outpost line of resistance, while the others rested along the main line of resistance. This latter tactic induced the enemy to expose his flank.

Right: In the interwoven roots of this tree on Guadalcanal, US marines discovered the bodies of three Japanese snipers killed by artillery fire. These densely entangled trees were a favourite hiding place for Japanese snipers.

Below: A Japanese soldier killed while lying in wait for enemy tanks, prepared to act as a 'human mine' by detonating the aerial bomb clutched to his chest as a tank rolled over him. This photograph is from Mektila in Burma in 1944.

Advanced Position Garrison

The garrison of the advanced position normally came from the troops assigned to the outpost position or from those of the main battle position, reinforced by machine guns and anti-tank weapons. Artillery elements were assigned support missions. Artillery was positioned in depth behind the main line of resistance so as to be able to mass its fire in support of the main positions in the area of the hostile probable main effort. One or two artillery companies

Reserve forces were normally held out by all units from the company upwards for the purpose of executing counter-attacks. The division reserve generally varied in size from one to three battalions. Its position was initially from 5029–5944m (5500–6500yd) in the rear of the main line of resistance, and was located in a sheltered position conveniently situated with respect to the probable area of counter-attack by the division. Japanese commanders normally attached tanks to reserve forces.

On the defensive, in fact, Japanese commanders usually placed their tanks in division reserve, under the cover of artillery fire and attack from the air by enemy aircraft. Eventually, tanks were attached to the infantry which had been assigned the counter-attack. Contrary to the generally held opinion that the Japanese rarely used armour in combat, tanks were very much part of offensive and especially defensive operations.

Tanks were considered to be extremely vital in stopping enemy mechanised forces, if the latter were to outrun their overhead artillery support or became dispersed. On occasion, Japanese commanders employed tanks in a raid on the hostile assembly area before the enemy could launch an attack. This was done by Japanese forces on Peleliu in September 1944, when a detachment of Japanese tanks sought to disrupt the Marine attack then in progress by attacking its reserve and division command post areas. In any case, tank attacks were mutually supported by overhead artillery support which neutralised American or British anti-tank guns.

Conduct of the Defence

As for the actual conduct of the defence, the advanced elements were the first forces encountered by an attacking enemy formation along outpost or advanced defensive positions. These forward defence elements conducted themselves in accordance with their overall mission, which was to delay or to impede an enemy attack. Artillery companies were assigned the mission of delaying the hostile force's advance, covering the withdrawal of friendly infantry or mechanised forces, and then falling back to prepared positions in the artillery zone where they reverted to the control of their organic commander.

As for the actual defence of the main line of resistance, as the enemy's hostile infantry formed up for the attack on the main line of resistance, the defensive artillery brought down its counter-battery fires. Tanks were then sent forwards, covered by artillery in order to upset or to disrupt the enemy's ability to continue the attack. As the enemy forces entered the pre-planned zones of infantry fire, sector commanders conducted the defence of their

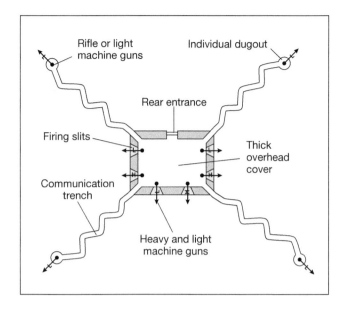

Above: A diagram showing an overhead view of a typical Japanese Army pillbox and the trench structure dug to provide it with support. Soldiers in the trenches outside could prevent enemy troops approaching close enough to knock out the pillbox.

sectors first by fire, then by the use of bayonets, in order to repulse the attacking enemy. The Japanese unhesitatingly counterattacked when the integrity of their position was threatened by enemy attack. Artillery assisted the close-in defence by standing barrages and concentrations brought down within the defensive position.

When it came to the timing of counter-attacks or counter-offensives, as the Japanese preferred to label them, division commanders were constantly on the alert in order to determine the proper time for the division counter-attack to commence. As experienced by US and British forces in the Pacific theatres, the Japanese preferred to launch a counter-attack when their attacks became bogged down (often because of stubborn resistance); when they walked into a well-prepared defensive zone; whenever a favourable situation arose on the battlefield due mainly to a successful counter-attack; or whenever the US and Allied forces paused to regroup or resupply. It was at this point that Japanese commanders set about plans to return to the offensive with the counter-attack aimed at envelopment or, as often encountered by US Marines throughout the Central Pacific, a massive frontal assault. Both artillery and tanks supported Japanese counter-attacks.

Japanese regulations discouraged defensive operations. As a result, commanders had a difficult time in restraining younger officers – normally platoon, company and battalion commanders – from assuming an offensive posture during defensive operations. This was especially the case on Iwo Jima in March 1945, where US Marines finally broke Japanese resistance after a subordinate disobeyed orders and launched a suicidal *banzai* or frontal assault against the Marines, who annihilated the attackers with artillery, machine-gun and rifle fire. In fact, due to this transgression, the Marines were able to finally penetrate the interlocking Japanese defences on Iwo Jima. This attack demonstrated that Japanese officers always had offensive operations uppermost in their minds and were quick, often hasty, to launch both large and small coordinated and uncoordinated counter-attacks on the slightest provocation. The disobedience of Japanese officers on Iwo Jima was expected, as, during pre-war manoeuvres, Japanese troops often abandoned their prearranged defensive positions in order to meet the attacker with the bayonet in front of their trenches or defensive positions.

Besides the large-sized unit defensive positions, the Japanese soldier employed individual defensive methods that were quite effective in delaying an enemy's advance. Lieutenant Colonel Frisbee, Executive Officer, 7th Marine

Regiment on Guadalcanal noted: 'The Japanese oftentimes set up their outposts in trees. I saw one tree which was rotten inside. The Japanese had a light machine gun and gunner down inside, and they had built a trap door on our side. Every once in a while the door would open, and they would poke the machine gun out and fire. We took care of this. When we cease firing, they cease firing. When we fire, they open up. They do this to conceal their positions.'

ISLAND AND ATOLL DEFENCES

There were two different types of defensive measure set up by the Japanese to deal with the 'island hopping' campaigns of Admiral Nimitz and General MacArthur during the latter part of World War II. These included atoll and island defences. Each of these two varieties of

Below: In Burma, a rare sight as a Japanese soldier surrenders to a member of the British 7th Division in 1944/45. As the war turned against Japan, the number of Japanese prisoners rose, but most still preferred to die rather than face capture and disgrace.

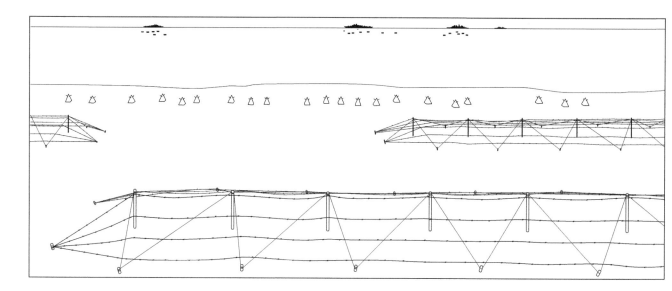

defence would entail different requirements in order to repel or defeat an enemy landing operation.

Atoll Defences

Atolls were low-lying islets enclosed with a lagoon which ran anywhere from 3.2km to 105km (2–65 miles) in diameter. These islets extended from a few metres to a few kilometres in length to several kilometres in width. Total land area of a typical atoll in the Central Pacific area ranged from a few hundred square metres to 10km (6 miles) in length. They were rarely more than 7.6m (25ft) above sea

Above: In order to counter a US Marine landing, the Japanese devised an elaborate system of beach defences. This 'defender's eye' view shows the barbed wire defences, and beyond them the mined anti-landing craft defences intended to disrupt a landing.

level, were covered by dense scrub brush and coconut or palm trees, and were bordered by salt marshes. The water table was normally only a few feet below the ground, thus negating the use of extensive trench or dug-in positions. Here, the Japanese normally built pillboxes and fortified bunkers. Despite the limitations placed upon the digging

of extensive trench lines, Japanese soldiers constructed anti-tank ditches and slit trenches that permitted riflemen to position themselves in the defence.

Japanese defence structures followed no set pattern, but were made, in general, to conform to the surrounding terrain in order to meet the immediate tactical requirements. With only a few exceptions, most defensive structures were flat and extended no more than 1–1.5m (3–5ft) above ground level, or were irregularly shaped and built around a base of trees. Japanese manuals on field fortifications stated: 'it was most important not to adhere blindly to set forms in construction work, but to adapt such work to fit the tactical situation'.

When the Japanese Army was forced to take up defensive positions, it adhered to the basic rule that construction of defensive positions involved a continual process of development. Starting out as a foxhole, fighting hole or slit trench, these were eventually linked to form a coordinated defence system. The third stage involved construction of strongpoints, bunker and pillbox types of earthworks, and log positions.

Japanese Defensive Positions

Japanese positions included bunkers, pillboxes, dugouts, shelters, blockhouses, rifle and machine-gun emplacements, foxholes, trenches and anti-aircraft emplacements, and revetments.

Above: Dead Japanese soldiers line a trench on Namur island, part of Kwajalein Atoll in the Marshall Islands. Few prisoners were taken here, as those who were not killed in battle took their own lives by committing hara-kiri.

Bunkers were normally found in those areas where high water-levels precluded the digging of deep trenches and in more or less open terrain, such as coconut tree groves or sugarcane fields, and on the edges of airfields. The finished interiors of bunkers varied from sizes of 1.2–1.8m (4–6ft) in height, 1.8–3m (6–10ft) in width, and 3.7–9.1m (12–30 feet) in length. Larger bunkers had two bays or compartments that were separated by a large, solid block of earth. Each bunker had one or more narrow firing slits for machine guns. As the Marines discovered on landing, the neutralisation of these bunkers proved difficult, as rifle fire often could not penetrate the narrow firing ports. The Japanese covered these slits up with some form of camouflage when not in use.

As US and Australian soldiers likewise discovered on Buna in New Guinea, the bunkers and pillboxes (the latter referred to as small bunkers) were built around the same general lines. With a shallow trench as a foundation, log columns and beams were erected, log revetment walls constructed, and a ceiling made of several layers of logs, laid laterally to the trench. With the completion of this basic superstructure, the revetment walls were reinforced

Left: 'The Price of Victory'. A member of the US Marine 4th Division lies dead on the sands of Iwo Jima after being shot in the head by intense Japanese sniper fire. Snipers were a constant and unwelcome threat to Allied landing forces.

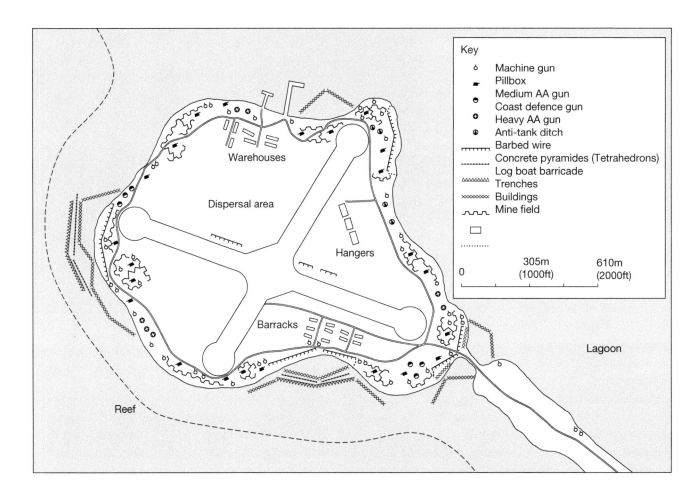

Key

○	Machine gun
▬	Pillbox
●	Medium AA gun
●	Coast defence gun
⊕	Heavy AA gun
⊕	Anti-tank ditch
┈┈┈	Barbed wire
··········	Concrete pyramides (Tetrahedrons)
	Log boat barricade
⋀⋀⋀⋀	Trenches
✕✕✕✕	Buildings
⌐╜╜╜	Mine field
▭	
··········	

0   305m (1000ft)   610m (2000ft)

Warehouses

Dispersal area

Hangers

Barracks

Lagoon

Reef

Above: A typical Japanese-controlled atoll in the Pacific, showing the extensive and varied defensive preparations against any Allied landing. At the centre of the atoll is the all-important airfield which would make this an important target for the Allies.

by such materials as sheets of iron, oil drums, ammunition boxes filled with sand, and additional piles of logs. The outside of the bunker was covered with dirt, rocks, coconuts and short pieces of logs. Camouflage of these bunkers consisted of a painted exterior with fast-growing vines and other types of vegetation.

The defence of a beach on an atoll was centred on the machine gun and a final protective line. The defence consisted of a shallow line of strongpoints with a secondary line of lesser density defences located slightly to the rear of the main defences. Because of the small size of atolls, the depth of the defence was limited. Strongpoints consisted of a group of bunkers and pillboxes, connected by communication trenches and in mutual support of each other. Each rifleman who was assigned to protect the pillbox or bunker had several alternative positions to carry out his mission. As the situation warranted, the Japanese infantryman ran from position to position. This often led to much confusion among Marine and US Army commanders and troops as to the actual strength of the defenders. In such positions, Japanese infantrymen made extensive use of hand-grenades particularly in the defence of small islands such as Tarawa and Makin in the Gilberts, and Kwajalein, Eniwetok and Roi-Namur in the Marshalls.

Disrupting an Attack

Japanese defence of these small islands was based on the idea of breaking up an attack before it reached the shore, and all coast guns up to 203mm (8in) calibre were sited so that they could be employed against small boats, landing craft and any amphibian vehicles carrying assault troops. Coastal and land batteries had local fire-director control, with two or three guns positioned with observation towards various gun positions to give mutual support. Flat trajectory weapons were used extensively by the Japanese, in contrast to indirect howitzer-type weapons which were rarely, if at all, used. The guns were placed well forwards on the beach where direct fire was then targeted against the approaching landing craft. Their grouping was shallow and all weapons were sited with the distinct mission of defeating the seaborne assault at the water's edge. In this capacity, the Japanese also used anti-aircraft guns to repel surface craft and landing vehicles.

As for the types and calibres of gun used, the Japanese normally employed 76mm (3in) to 203mm (8in) guns. The 203mm guns were usually in turrets, while the 127mm (5in) and 152mm (6in) guns were separate field pieces protected by shields. All of these guns were placed in heavy revetments, with ammunition for the weapons being stored in covered emplacements near the guns. Machine guns were situated so as to fire outwards around the perimeter. Most of these weapons were positioned for crossfire and covered the beaches with enfilading fire. A few were situated to fire to the rear of their positions in case the enemy had managed to achieve a breakthrough elsewhere and were encircling the guns. Some machine guns were situated in open emplacements, while others machine guns were set up in pillboxes.

Those located in the open pillboxes were generally dual purpose and had wide fields of fire, while those situated in enclosed pillboxes had a much narrower field of fire. These latter machine-gun positions were situated to fire in only one direction. All emplacements were protected by riflemen positioned in foxholes and trenches around the fortifications. Some positions were defended by howitzers and trench mortars, although on Tarawa, because the *Rikusentai* had few of these weapons, they instead employed howitzers in the defence of such positions.

Field Fortifications

Japanese defence of the small islands or atolls was characterised by an extensive use of field fortifications, which in turn prompted a change in US Marine tactics and organisation in dealing with them. After Tarawa, US Marine units organised special assault teams of 'bunker-busters' that employed the method called 'Find'em, fix'em and blast'em', which had the task of dealing specifically with Japanese bunkers. The machine guns were the centre of these bunker and pillbox defences. These fortifications ranged from simple fortifications of palm logs and sand manned by two to three men, to the more extensive versions made of concrete and steel, and manned by a squad of soldiers. As the Japanese Army was forced increasingly onto the defensive, American forces encountered more of the latter heavily reinforced defences. Built with concrete and steel, they were relatively safe from most smaller calibre shells and could only be destroyed either by larger calibre guns or, as was normally the case, by teams of Marines or soldiers armed with satchel charges

Below: A Japanese pillbox reinforced with coconut logs and covered with sand on Tarawa in November 1943. Coconut logs were a common material featured in many Japanese bunkers in the Pacific.

of TNT and gasoline drums, flame-throwers, bazookas and small arms fire (this was the so-called 'corkscrew' method of 'Blast'em and burn'em').

The Japanese defended these positions to the last man, with some defenders living amid the decomposing corpses of their comrades, only to come out a few days after the island had been declared secured, bearing a machine gun or hand-grenade and inflicting casualties on the Marines or soldiers. This was especially the case on Tarawa and Makin in November 1943.

One last point concerning Japanese fighting techniques during the World War II was the fact that, if the Japanese were unable to stop an amphibious assault before it hit the beach and landed Marines or soldiers, these beach strongpoints in every case were eventually overrun, thus nullifying the scheme of overall defence. In order to launch a counter-attack, at least according to its offensive doctrine, infantrymen were withdrawn from their pillboxes and formed into assault detachments, thus losing the advantage in firepower from fixed defensive positions. This procedure and the counter-attack that inevitably followed were in line with the Japanese Army's normal tactical doctrine.

Whenever their lines of bunkers and pillboxes were breached, the remaining Japanese troops usually broke up into small groups and withdrew into covered areas, where they re-formed and counterattacked. When these counter-attacks were broken up, they then formed into small groups

---

Below: Dead Japanese soldiers lie in front of a burned out bunker. US Marines and soldiers had to blast and burn the Japanese out of these emplacements using flamethrowers, explosives, and a heavy weight of supporting fire.

to take refuge in bunkers, air-raid shelters, slit trenches or saltmarsh jungles while US or Allied troops 'mopped up'. This was the point at which many Japanese soldiers chose suicide, rather than capture and loss of face. Some remnants of their forces hid for days after the fighting had stopped, subsisting on coconuts and captured enemy rations. In one rather humorous incident on Bougainville in the Northern Solomons, Japanese soldiers were known to have joined the Marines to watch the nightly movie! Usually, however, Japanese soldiers largely either committed suicide or attempted to flee the area to neighbouring islands, where many remained until they were repatriated back to Japan at the end of the war.

Pillboxes

Pillboxes were constructed over or near dugouts to which Japanese soldiers could flee for protection while being shelled or bombed. Some had front and rear compartments, the front part for firing and the rear for protection, storage or supplies, and rest and sleep. Some of the dugouts were as much as 3m (10ft) deep or more. Like bunkers, they had narrow slits for enfilading machine-gun fire and proved just as difficult to neutralise. They were constructed with sand-filled gasoline drums placed at intervals in front of trenches, with enough space left to allow automatic weapons and rifle fire from inside by the defenders. Heavy palm logs were piled 1–1.5m (3–5ft) in front of the drums in such a way that they did not block the loopholes for firing. The structure was then covered with sod and camouflaged by shrubs or scrub brush, planted to provide excellent cover and concealment.

On Tarawa, Japanese pillboxes, blockhouses, open and covered trenches, and open revetments formed the main defensive system. The Japanese situated these structures and fortifications within 91m (100yd) of the high-tide mark on the beaches. The pillboxes were constructed mainly of reinforced concrete (several of which were measured to be almost 406mm (16in) thick), coconut palm logs and sand. Steel pillboxes shaped as hexagons (six-sided) were used as command posts. These resembled pyramids from the outside and were found on all the beaches. They had been prefabricated and emplaced by the labour troops (Formosans (Taiwanese) and Koreans) and were designed to serve as command and observation posts.

The pillboxes found on Tarawa had double walls, between which sand and other material were placed for added protection. As the Marines discovered once they landed, most of the beach defence guns on that island (Betio, part of the Tarawa atoll) were emplaced in dugouts with

Above: On Tarawa, dead Japanese soldiers lie amidst the carnage of battle. Note that the Japanese had elected to make a Banzai charge against the Marines, despite their prepared defensive positions, thus fatally weakening the defence of the island.

overhead protection that rendered naval gunfire and close air support almost totally useless in the absence of a direct hit. Many of these dugouts were made of reinforced concrete. As British troops discovered during the fighting in Burma, Japanese pillboxes in the jungles were very similar to those found in the South and Central Pacific areas. Both types of pillbox and bunker were designed for use by any of the weapons utilised by the Japanese Army Infantry Regiment, although they were primarily used for the 37mm (1.47in) anti-tank guns and heavy machine guns.

Island Defences

On volcanic islands such as Peleliu, Iwo Jima and Okinawa, the defence normally consisted of beach positions, heavy and naval gun emplacements of up to 305mm (12in) guns, and mobile infantry reserves. Beach defences included obstacles such as barbed or concertina wire, coconut logs and anti-tank obstacles. As British and American troops discovered in their various landing operations in Burma and the South and Central Pacific, the Japanese situated these beach defences as well forward

of the assault line as possible. As the war shifted from one of offensive to defensive operations, the Japanese correspondingly shifted their tactical response in meeting the overwhelming Allied superiority in men and materiel. Whereas at Tarawa, the attacking Marines met fanatical Japanese resistance at the water's edge, these tactics gave way – ironically at the advice of their German allies – to allowing the landing to occur with only minimal resistance. This was in order to draw the attacking forces inland and then, through a mobile defence, systematically defeat them. The Japanese began to employ such tactics during the landings on Saipan in June 1944. After the Marines proceeded inland about 1.6km (1 mile) from the beachhead in amphibious assault vehicles or amtracs, Japanese artillery and machine guns pummelled them, with the result that only a few managed to continue the

advance. As the Saipan operation continued, Japanese tank–infantry teams, pillboxes and extensive interlocking defences forced the Marines to slug it out yard by yard against these new Japanese tactics.

These same tactics were present on Peleliu in September 1944, as the Marines and US Army came up against fanatical Japanese resistance, which forced them to fight for every square inch of the island. It was on Iwo Jima, however, that the full effect of these new Japanese tactics was felt, as the Marines once again came across fanatical resistance from an enemy whom they could not see. Dug into volcanic terrain surrounding Mt Suribachi, the Japanese defenders lobbed shells onto the Marines as they attempted to move off the beach towards Suribachi and beyond. Defended by 21,000 seasoned Japanese soldiers and commanded by perhaps one of the best generals of World War II, General Tadamichi Kuribayashi, the Japanese infantrymen made the Marines pay in blood for every inch they advanced inland. As Marine Private Richard Allen recounted, his Marine outfit, the 1st Battalion, 28th Marines, incurred almost 50 per cent casualties after only one-and-a-half days of combat, in fighting that was 'vicious … [and in many instances] … hand to hand'. Private Allen added that Marine patrols 'spent much of the day (and campaign) destroying pillboxes and emplacements bypassed the previous day (D-Day – 19 February 1945)'. Making extensive use of the 'corkscrew method', Marine assault teams (a flame-thrower, Browning Automatic riflemen and satchel charge) and combat engineers were

Above: A Japanese Type 95 Light Tank used as a pillbox on Eniwetok atoll in the Pacific. Dug in in this manner, a tank could prove a formidable obstacle to any attacking troops, and was best knocked out by artillery or air strike.

forced to blast and burn the Japanese out of their earthen fortresses. General Kuribayashi, a skilled and resourceful officer hand-picked to defend Iwo Jima, realised that the Americans would attack with maximum force. He thus decided that, instead of meeting the Americans on the beachhead, he would wait until they were firmly ashore and then counterattack. Holed up in caves dug into the mountainside, the Japanese poured unremitting fire on the Marines. Only after nearly one-and-a-half months of fighting, and at the cost of 5500 Marines, was Iwo Jima secured. On only two occasions, near the end of the campaign, did Marines actually see Japanese soldiers attacking them. This occurred when a subordinate disobeyed General Kuribayashi's order forbidding frontal assaults against the attackers. In the *banzai* charges that followed, the Marines slaughtered the Japanese as they aimed for the rear area of the Americans.

This same scheme of defence was used by the Japanese on Okinawa in April 1945, as both the US Marines and Army discovered during the three-month campaign. As on Iwo Jima, the Japanese withdrew to a fortified line known as the Shuri Castle Line, which consisted of a series of interlocking, well-prepared defences. Here, the Japanese fought the Americans to a standstill for nearly three months. Nearly 100,000 Japanese defenders were killed in a battle of attrition that served as a powerful reminder as to what the Allies could expect if they were to invade the Japanese Home Islands.

JUNGLE WARFARE

One last method of offensive warfare practised by the Japanese was jungle warfare. The Japanese enjoyed remarkable success during the first two years of World War II in the Pacific, against the British in Malaya, Singapore and Burma, against the Americans in the Philippines, and in the early phases of the New Guinea campaign. Prior to the start of World War II, the Japanese had trained extensively for this type of warfare. Despite their lack of motorised vehicles and their orientation towards fighting in the type of terrain found in China and the USSR, Japanese forces proved quite adept at fighting in the jungles. Over time, they gained a considerable reputation for their ability to overcome equipment and

Below: Two US soldiers advance against a fortified Japanese position located in a cave on Okinawa. By preparing defensive positions in caves, the Japanese were protected from shelling or aerial bombardment, and Marines were forced to take each one.

logistical shortages. However, this myth of 'invincibility' was shattered as both the British under Field Marshal William Slim's 14th Army in Burma and General Douglas MacArthur's soldiers and Marines became adept at fighting in the jungle.

SUMMARY

US Army and Marine intelligence reports suggested that after World War II, 'Japanese conduct of the defense was characterized by tenacity and a determination to fight to the last man and the last round.' As US soldiers discovered after 1943, 'any attacking force which gains a foothold in a Japanese coastal defense position must expect to meet concentrated and accurate fire from flanking strongpoints and must be ready to withstand an immediate and determined counterattack'. Among the main weaknesses of the Japanese in repelling such an assault was the inability to adapt themselves to the unexpected; their coast defence positions were found to be extremely vulnerable to surprise, either in the nature or direction of attack. However, the Japanese use of defence tactics can still be characterised as tenacious and displaying a willingness to fight to the last man and round: any US or British landing against the Japanese discovered that they were effective in responding with concentrated and accurate fire from flanking strongpoints in an immediate and determined counter-attack.

Japanese defence tactics likewise prompted organisational and tactical procedure changes inside the US Marine division after Tarawa in 1943. Faced with imminent invasions on all of its island possessions, the Japanese High Command shifted from a static line defence to a gradual war of attrition aimed at wearing down the Americans. The construction of insular fortifications and a defence-in-depth situated away from the beachhead forced the Marines to create special assault teams equipped with explosives and flame weapons in order to 'Find'em, fix'em and blast'em'. As the assaults from Peleliu to Okinawa demonstrated, the Japanese were determined to make the Americans pay in blood for every inch of Japanese-held soil they conquered.

CHAPTER 5

Small Arms and Equipment of the Japanese Soldier

Overall, the quality of Japanese equipment in World War II was not as good as that of the enemy. Many of the small arms were derived from World War I-vintage European weapons, and they used a wide variety of ammunition, causing logistical problems for the armed forces.

LIKE HIS AMERICAN AND BRITISH counterpart, the Japanese soldier's ability to fight depended largely upon the equipment issued to him in order to carry out his mission. From his battle-drab uniform to his Nambu 8mm (0.315in) pistol and Model 38 Arisaka rifle, the Japanese soldier was well equipped to carry out his assigned missions throughout World War II. The following is a brief description of his uniform and kit, his small arms (pistols and rifles), machine guns, mortars and grenades and grenade launchers.

UNIFORMS

There were two distinct types of Japanese uniforms worn during World War II in temperate zones, and a separate one for colder climates such as Manchuria and China proper. The majority of Japanese soldiers wore the M-1930 coat, made of a heavy, mustard-coloured woollen cloth, with a stand-up collar, to which the insignia of the arm and unit the soldier belonged was affixed, except when in the field. The most common Japanese soldier's uniform seen by US and British troops in the Pacific War was the M-1938 coat, which was olive drab in colour and made from either cotton or wool, depending on the season and had a turn-down collar and four pockets with flaps.

In the field, the Japanese wore ordinary semi-breeches, cut high in the waist and held up by two webbing straps. Wrapped spiral puttees were normally won by dismounted enlisted men. Officers likewise wore puttees, boots or leather leggings, with either breeches or semi-breeches. Long trousers without cuffs were worn with the M-1930 coat, but were covered with puttees, boots or leggings.

As for headgear, the Japanese wore a field cover, a steel helmet or a service cap. The field cap with its narrow visor was made of olive-drab woollen cloth and fashioned according to the shape of the head. It had a brown leather chin strap and a star along the vertical front seams, and was sometimes worn underneath the helmet. In most instances, specifically in more tropical climates, a piece of cloth was attached to the back of the hat to protect the neck from the sun. During combat operations, however, Japanese soldiers wore steel helmets, with webbing tapes tied under the chin or at the back of the neck and the star insignia affixed to the front. However, being made of a light steel alloy, the helmets were of poor quality and easily pierced by a bullet or fragment. The service cap was worn exclusively by officers and mostly in garrison. Its shape resembled that of the US Army, US Marine Corps and British officer's service cap. It was made of wool and was olive-drab in colour, with red piping to denote the officer ranks.

Left: Japanese troops stand ready to move out in China in 1938. They hold their Arisaka rifles in their right hand and carry their equipment on their backs. The soldier in the foreground has used two flags to provide extra space for his kit.

For footwear, Japanese enlisted men wore hobnailed service shoes made of pigskin or cowhide with a metal-rimmed heel. Officers' boots and shoes were of similar design, but were black. All Japanese soldiers carried an extra pair of shoes – rubber-soled, black canvas *tabi* – for warm weather. Most *tabi* had metal cleats under the ball of the foot for better traction in the jungles or on rugged terrain.

Rank insignia was worn on the collar and sleeves of the blouse or tunic. Soldiers were issued raincoats, but most preferred to wear the shelter half or poncho for rain protection. Most were issued cotton or light-wool underwear; the undershirt or breech clout was sometimes worn as a blouse in tropical climates. All soldiers were issued a *Senninbari* '1000 stitch good luck belt', a red sash with 1000 stitches worn for good luck and 'immunity from enemy fire'.

The Japanese soldier was equipped for quick, swift movement. His field equipment or battle kit consisted of a field pack of heavy duck material about 330mm (13in) square and 127mm (5in) deep. Inside the pack, the soldier carried a pair of shoes (usually the *tabi*), a shelter half with poles and pins, socks, towel, soap, toiletries, sewing kit, first-aid kit, a breech clout and several days' rations. Attached around the outside of the pack was a blanket or overcoat rolled into a horseshoe shape, with a raincoat or shelter half across the top. The mess kit was strapped to the back. A hold-all or light canvas bag was carried on the back or slung over the shoulder. The Japanese soldier also carried numerous bags that contained grenades, extra ammunition and, sometimes, special equipment. Also attached to the field pack was an entrenching tool that consisted of either a short-handled shovel or a pick.

In addition to the mess kit, shelter half and canteens, the Japanese soldier wore an ammunition belt around the waist with attached ammunition pouches, with two smaller pouches worn in the front and a larger one in the rear below the pack. The bayonet and bayonet frog were likewise worn on the ammunition belt. At the start of World War II, the standard-issue ammunition belt was made of leather. However, as the war progressed, the Japanese introduced a new rubberised fabric belt that was water resistant, making it ideal for use in the subtropical areas of the South Pacific and the Burmese jungles.

INFANTRY WEAPONS

Like his field equipment, the Japanese soldier carried a vast array of infantry weapons, many of which had their antecedents with American, German, British and Russian equipment. This section is a brief overview of individual weapons which were carried by the Japanese soldier during World War II.

Pistols

Nambu 8mm Pistol

The Nambu 8mm Pistol was a semi-automatic, recoil-operated, magazine-fed hand-held weapon.

■ CALIBRE: 8mm (0.315in); MAGAZINE CAPACITY: 8 rounds; WEIGHT: 0.88kg (1lb 15oz) empty; MUZZLE VELOCITY: 290m/s (950ft/s)

Model 26 9mm Revolver

The Model 26 (1893) Revolver was a copy of the Smith and Wesson six-chambered, double-action weapon, and it was reputed among the Japanese Army to be of questionable accuracy.

■ CALIBRE: 9mm (0.38in); MAGAZINE CAPACITY: 6 rounds; WEIGHT: 1.13kg (2lb 8oz); OVERALL LENGTH: 216mm (8.5in); MUZZLE VELOCITY: 229m/s (750ft/s)

Below: Japanese troops armed with a Type 100 flamethrower attack an American bunker position on Bataan in the Philippines in 1942. The other members of the squad stand ready to advance after the flames have eliminated the defenders.

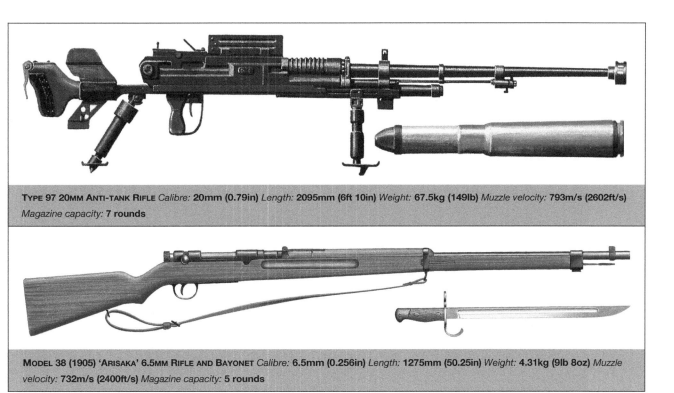

TYPE 97 20MM ANTI-TANK RIFLE *Calibre:* **20mm (0.79in)** *Length:* **2095mm (6ft 10in)** *Weight:* **67.5kg (149lb)** *Muzzle velocity:* **793m/s (2602ft/s)** *Magazine capacity:* **7 rounds**

MODEL 38 (1905) 'ARISAKA' 6.5MM RIFLE AND BAYONET *Calibre:* **6.5mm (0.256in)** *Length:* **1275mm (50.25in)** *Weight:* **4.31kg (9lb 8oz)** *Muzzle velocity:* **732m/s (2400ft/s)** *Magazine capacity:* **5 rounds**

Rifles
Model No. 38 (1905) 'Arisaka' 6.5mm Rifle
This was a manually operated, clip-loaded, magazine-fed rifle with a Mauser-type bolt action, most commonly referred to as the Arisaka. A less-common carbine version was issued at the same time.
■ CALIBRE: 6.5mm (0.256in); MAGAZINE CAPACITY: 5 rounds; WEIGHT: 4.31kg (9lb 8oz); LENGTH: 1275mm (50.25in); MUZZLE VELOCITY: 732m/s (2400ft/s)

Model No. 44 (1911) Cavalry Carbine
This was essentially the same as the Arisaka (1905) carbine. All of the rifle's actions are similar to those of the Model 38 Arisaka, although it had a spike bayonet that folded underneath and rested in a slot in the stock. The rifle used the same ammunition as the Model 38, with both ball and tracer ammunition.
■ CALIBRE: 6.5mm (0.256in); MAGAZINE CAPACITY: 5 rounds; WEIGHT: 3.9kg (8 3/4 lb); LENGTH: 972mm (38.25in); MUZZLE VELOCITY: 685m/s (2250ft/s)

Model 99 (1939) 7.7mm Rifle
This improved version of the Model 38 Arisaka with its heavier calibre began entering service in 1939. The Japanese Army issued this service rifle to regular infantry and service troops. Its ammunition could be used in the Model 92 machine gun.

■ CALIBRE: 7.7mm (0.303in); MAGAZINE CAPACITY: 5 rounds; WEIGHT: 3.99kg (8.8lb); LENGTH: 1118mm (44in); MUZZLE VELOCITY: 701m/s (2300ft/s)

Model No. 97 6.5mm Sniper's Rifle
The Japanese used two distinct types of sniper rifle during World War II: the Model No. 97 (1937) 6.5mm and Model No. 99 (1939) rifles, both distinguished from the standard infantry weapons by their telescopic sights.
■ CALIBRE: (Model 97) 6.5mm (0.256in); (Model 99) 7.7mm (0.303in); WEIGHT: 4.42kg (9.75lb) with scope, (both models); TELESCOPIC SIGHTS: Type: fixed focus; Magnification: 2.5x; Field of vision: 10 degrees; Weight: 0.48kg (17oz)

Machine Guns
The Japanese Army, like its British and American enemies, was armed with a vast array of light- and heavy machine guns. The basic machine gun was the 'Nambu' Model 11 6.5mm (0.256in) light machine gun, based on the French Hotchkiss. Other guns copied were the Lewis, Vickers and, in some instances, the Oerlikon. It is important to note that for some reason the Japanese neglected submachine gun development. The Type 100 submachine gun was not a success and was not issued in large numbers. Some MP40 'Schmeissers' and .30 calibre 'Solothurn' submachine guns were obtained from the Germans.

A Japanese soldier carrying the Type 100 submachine gun. The gun was difficult to manufacture and in short supply.

Model No. 11 (1922) 6.5mm Light Machine Gun
This was a gas-operated, air-cooled machine gun with a hopper feed which held 6 5-round clips of ammunition.
■ CALIBRE: 6.5mm (0.256in); HOPPER CAPACITY: 6
5-round clips; WEIGHT: 10.2kg (22lb 8oz); LENGTH:

1044mm (43.5in); MUZZLE VELOCITY: 744m/s (2440ft/s);
RATE OF FIRE: 500rpm

Model No. 96 (1936) 6.5mm Light Machine Gun
This was a gas-operated, air-cooled, magazine-fed full automatic light machine gun. Its appearance is very similar to that of the British Bren light machine gun.
■ CALIBRE: 6.5mm (0.256mm); MAGAZINE: 30 rounds;
WEIGHT: 9.07kg (20lb) without bayonet or magazine;
LENGTH: 1054mm (41.5in): MUZZLE VELOCITY: 735m/s
(2410ft/s); RATE OF FIRE: 550rpm

Model No. 99 (1939) 7.7mm Light Machine Gun
This was a gas-operated, magazine-fed, air-cooled light machine gun.
■ CALIBRE: 7.7mm (0.303in); MAGAZINE: 30 rounds;
WEIGHT: 10.43kg (23lb); LENGTH: 1181m (46.5in); MUZZLE
VELOCITY: 715m/s (2350ft/s); RATE OF FIRE: 850rpm

Model No. 92 (1932) 7.7mm Heavy Machine Gun
Modelled on the French Hotchkiss, this was the standard Japanese heavy machine gun used in the Pacific during World War II.
■ CALIBRE: 7.7mm (0.303in); STRIP CAPACITY: 30 rounds;
WEIGHT: 55.34kg (122lb); LENGTH: 1156mm (45.5in);
MUZZLE VELOCITY: 732m/s (2400ft/s); RATE OF FIRE: 450rpm

Model No. 93 (1933) 13mm Heavy Machine Gun
This was a gas-operated, air-cooled, full automatic Hotchkiss type anti-aircraft gun. It was magazine-fed and was used by the Japanese primarliy against troops and light-skinned enemy vehicles.
■ CALIBRE: 13.2mm (0.52in); MAGAZINE: 30 rounds;
WEIGHT: 39kg (87lb); LENGTH: 2.26m (89in); MUZZLE
VELOCITY: 686m/s (2250ft/s); RATE OF FIRE: 450rpm

Mortars
Model No. 10 (1921) 50mm Grenade Discharger
This was a smooth-bore, muzzle-loaded weapon which was used primarily for discharging flares. The heavier Model No. 89 grenade discharger was used for firing high explosives and other projectiles.
■ CALIBRE: 50mm; WEIGHT: 2.5kg (5.5lb); LENGTH OF
BARREL: 241mm (9.5in); OVERALL LENGTH: 508mm (20in);
RANGE: 59–160m (65–175yd) with M91 grenade

Model No. 89 (1929) 50mm Grenade Discharger
Commonly referred to as the 'knee mortar', the Model No. 89 50mm Grenade Discharger was a muzzle-fed,

rifled weapon which was widely used by the Japanese Army throughout World War II.
- CALIBRE: 50mm; WEIGHT: 4.7kg (10.5lb); LENGTH: 610mm (24in) overall; RANGE: 120–674m (131–737yd)

Model No. 98 (1938) 50mm Mortar

This was a smooth-bore, muzzle-loaded weapon with a fixed elevation of approximately 40 degrees. It fired a stick bomb of 4.5kg (10lb) containing 3.2kg (7lb) of picric acid.
- CALIBRE: 50mm; WEIGHT: 21.8kg (48lb); LENGTH: 635mm (25in); RANGE: 366m (400yd) approx

Model No. 99 (1939) 81mm Mortar

This was a smooth-bore, muzzle-loading, high-angle fire weapon derived from the earlier Model 97 mortar.
- CALIBRE: 81mm; WEIGHT: 23.6kg (52lb); LENGTH: 641.35mm (25.25in); RANGE: 2012m (2200yd)

Model No. 94 (1934) 90mm Mortar

This was a smooth-bore, muzzle-loading weapon with a fixed firing pin. Although a successful design, it was relatively uncommon in Japanese service.
- CALIBRE: 90mm; TOTAL WEIGHT: 154.2kg (340lb); LENGTH OF BARREL: 1214mm (47.8in); RANGE: 3795m (4150yd)

Model 93 (1933) 150mm Heavy Mortar

This was the heaviest calibre mortar in service with the Japanese Army during World War II. It threw a shell that weighed 25.4kg (56lb) and contained 6.4kg (14lb) of explosives. It was a smooth-bore, muzzle-loaded lanyard-fired weapon.
- CALIBRE: 150mm; WEIGHT OF TUBE: 99.8kg (220lb); LENGTH OF TUBE: 1.50m (59in); RANGE: 2103m (2300yd)

Grenades and Rifle Grenades

The following models of grenade were used to devastating effect against the Allied troops opposing them by Japanese infantrymen during the course of World War II.

Model No. 91
- LENGTH: 126mm (4.95in); DIAMETER: 50mm (1.97in); FUSE DELAY: 7–8 seconds; WEIGHT: 0.53kg (18.8oz); TYPE: Fragmentary

Model No. 97
- LENGTH: 95mm (3.75in); DIAMETER: 50mm (1.97in); FUSE DELAY: 4–5 seconds; WEIGHT: 0.45kg (1lb); TYPE: Fragmentary

Model No. 99
- LENGTH: 89mm (3.50in); DIAMETER: 42mm (1.65in); FUSE DELAY: 4–5 seconds; WEIGHT: 0.28kg (10oz); TYPE: Fragmentary

Model No. 23
- LENGTH: 95mm (3.75in); DIAMETER: 51mm (2in); FUSE DELAY: 4–5 seconds; WEIGHT: 0.45kg (1lb); TYPE: Fragmentary

One other type of grenade used by Japanese infantrymen during the course of World War II was the Japanese high-explosive stick-grenade. Similar in appearance to the German hand-grenade, which was commonly known as the 'potato masher', it weighed 0.54kg (19oz) and its length was 200mm (7.89in). Its fuse delay, like the three models listed above – the Model No. 97, the Model No. 99, and the Model No. 23 – was 4–5 seconds.

Below: Two Japanese soldiers man a Model 10 'Knee' Mortar in China. The small size of the mortar made it easily portable, but the weight of the shell fired was light, and had little explosive effect. It was therefore largely used to fire flares.

CHAPTER 6

Support Weapons of a Japanese Infantry Division

The Japanese infantry division, the main fighting unit of the Japanese armed forces, could call on a variety of support units to aid it in meeting its objectives. From artillery to armoured cars, and mortars to tanks, the Japanese were gradually outclassed by the quality of Allied equipment facing them.

THE JAPANESE ARMY OF WORLD WAR II was considered to have a primary function: to attack the enemy, not to defend Japanese territory. Japanese commanders and strategists knew that the Army was first and foremost an infantry-based force, but they also knew that during battle they had at their disposal a vast array of light- and medium tanks and artillery to support the infantry while they went forward in the attack. Whereas the American and British forces fought a primarily infantry-based war with Japan throughout the Pacific theatres, the Japanese Army had been organised to fight a mechanised war against the USSR.

Despite the fact that the Japanese Army was late in mechanising its forces, it nonetheless fielded fully mechanised units. In time, these mechanised units were to see extensive action in China against the forces of the Nationalist Chinese under Generalissimo Chiang Kai-Shek, and US and British forces in Burma, the Central and South Pacific, and on Okinawa. This section sets out to briefly examine the tanks and artillery pieces which were most frequently used by the Japanese Army and the Japanese special naval landing forces (*Rikusentai*) throughout the Pacific theatre during World War II.

Left: A Japanese Type 95 tank rumbles past a Buddhist temple in Rangoon, Burma. In the early years of the war the Allies did not possess significant anti-tank weaponry, which meant that Japanese armoured shortcomings were not exploited.

ARTILLERY

Infantry Guns

The following artillery pieces were standard to every infantry division in the Japanese Army. The mission of Japanese artillery was the support of the infantry while the infantry was engaged in an attack on the enemy and its positions, as well as when it was engaged in defence.

Model No. 94 (1934) 37mm Gun

The Model No. 94 (1934) gun, with its 37mm (1.47in) calibre, was commonly referred to by the Japanese Army and its soldiers as an 'infantry rapid fire gun'. This particular model served as a infantry support weapon and, as such, was capable of firing high-explosive and armour-piercing high-explosive shells.

■ CALIBRE: 37mm (1.47in); WEIGHT: 323.9kg (714lb); LENGTH: 2.90m (114in); RANGE: 4572m (5000yd); MUZZLE VELOCITY: 2103m (2300yd); AMMUNITION: High-explosive and armour-piercing

Model 1 (1941) 47mm Gun

The Model 1 (1941) Gun, with its 47mm (1.85in) calibre, was a modern anti-tank gun. As such, it was equipped with armour-piercing high-explosive shells, as well as the standard high-explosive shells.

■ CALIBRE: 47mm (1.85in); WEIGHT: 725.7kg (1600lb); BARREL LENGTH: 2.52m (99.4in); RANGE: 7680m (8400yd); MUZZLE VELOCITY: 823m/s (2700ft/s); AMMUNITION: High-explosive and armour-piercing

Above: A Model 92 (70mm) battalion level gun. Although visually unimpressive, the gun proved to be an excellent infantry support weapon. Due to its lack of range and rudimentary sighting system, it was used well forward, close to the enemy lines.

Model 92 (1932) 70mm Howitzer Battalion Gun

This model of howitzer battalion gun was one of the most effective and common infantry support weapons in the Japanese artillery arsenal.

■ CALIBRE: 70mm (2.75in); WEIGHT: 212.3kg (468lb); BARREL LENGTH: 0.72m (28.5in); RANGE: 2812m (3075yd); MUZZLE VELOCITY: 198m/s (650ft/s); AMMUNITION: High-explosive and smoke

Model 41 (1908) 75mm Infantry Gun

The Model 41 (1908) infantry gun was the standard infantry support pack howitzer for the Japanese Army. It performed this role until it was finally superseded by the Model 94 (1934) 75mm pack howitzer. The Model 41 was primarily used as a regimental infantry gun, and it would remain in service throughout World War II, used as an infantry support gun. It was popular with Japanese troops for the simple reason that it had one of the highest degrees of accuracy of any Japanese field gun.

■ CALIBRE: 75mm (2.95in); WEIGHT: 544.3kg (1200lb); LENGTH: 4.31m (170in); RANGE: 10,963m (11,990yd); MUZZLE VELOCITY: 198m/s (650ft/s); AMMUNITION: High-explosive, armour-piercing, shrapnel; hollow charge anti-personnel; incendiary

Field Artillery Guns
Model 94 (1934) 75mm Mountain Pack Howitzer

During World War II this was the standard Japanese pack or mountain artillery piece, which replaced the Model 41 mountain gun. It was designed specifically for rapid assembly and quick disassembly, and it would be transported to and from combat areas by six packhorses.

■ CALIBRE: 75mm (2.95in); WEIGHT: 544.3kg (1200lb); MAXIMUM RANGE: 8000m (8750yd); MAXIMUM RATE OF FIRE: 10–12rpm; AMMUNITION: High-explosive, antipersonnel, shrapnel, chemical, flare incendiary

Model 90 (1930) 75mm Gun

This gun became the standard Japanese Army field piece in 1936, and during this year, the weapon was issued to all divisions. Despite the fact that this 75mm (2.95in) calibre model arrived prewar, the enemies of the Japanese – the US, British and Chinese troops – did not encounter the effect of its fire during World War II until late on in the conflict.

■ CALIBRE: 75mm (2.95in); WEIGHT: 1497kg (3300lb); MAXIMUM RANGE: 15,000m (16,250yd); MAXIMUM RATE OF FIRE: 10–12rpm; AMMUNITION: High-explosive, antipersonnel, incendiary, flare

Model 95 (1935) 75mm Gun

The Model No. 95 (1935) gun was the standard Japanese field piece until superseded by the updated Model 90. This field piece, with its 75mm (2.95in) calibre, was used by several units in the Japanese Armed Forces, such as the *Rikusentai* (special landing forces), as well as various other specialised units.

■ CALIBRE: 75mm (2.95in); WEIGHT: 1105.9kg (2438lb); MAXIMUM RANGE: 11,000m (12,030yd); MUZZLE VELOCITY: 500m/s (1640ft/s); MAXIMUM RATE OF FIRE: 10–12rpm; AMMUNITION: High-explosive, antipersonnel, shrapnel, chemical

Model 14 (1925) 105mm Field Gun

This field piece was used for long-range firing. The Model 14 105mm (4.1in) Field Gun was tractor-drawn, as opposed to being horse-drawn, as were most Japanese field guns during World War II.

■ CALIBRE: 105mm (4.1in); WEIGHT: 3107kg (6850lb) in firing position; MAXIMUM RANGE: 13,259–15,088m (14,500–16,500yd); MAXIMUM RATE OF FIRE: 6–8rpm; AMMUNITION: High-explosive, shrapnel, smoke, incendiary, chemical

Model 91 (1931) 105mm Howitzer

This was a lightweight modern field howitzer that had a short barrel and long sleigh. It was towed by six horses.
■ CALIBRE: 105mm (4.1in); WEIGHT: 1927.8kg (4250lb) in firing position; MAXIMUM RANGE: 10,516m (11,500yd); MAXIMUM RATE OF FIRE: 6–8rpm; AMMUNITION: High-explosive, anti-personnel, chemical, armour-piercing, shrapnel

Model No. 92 (1932) 105mm Gun

This field artillery piece was used primarily for long-range firing. Unusually for Japanese field pieces, it was drawn by a tractor or a 5080kg (5 ton) truck.
■ CALIBRE: 105mm(4.1in); WEIGHT: 2993.7kg (6600lb) in firing position; MAXIMUM RANGE:14,996–18,288m (16,400–20,000yd); RATE OF FIRE: 6–8rpm; MUZZLE VELOCITY: 762m/s (2500ft/s); AMMUNITION: High-explosive, anti-personnel, smoke, incendiary, chemical

---

Below: A Model 41 gun in action in China in 1938. The Model 41 was a popular weapon because it had one of the highest degrees of accuracy of any Japanese field piece. Although replaced by the Model 94, they remained in service throughout the war.

Model No. 89 (1929) 150mm Heavy Field Howitzer

This was a tractor-drawn heavy howitzer which was designed primarily for long-range fire support and was designated a heavy field artillery piece. It was one of the most powerful field pieces used by the Japanese Army and was in service throughout the Pacific theatres, primarily in China and Burma, and on the island atolls in the Central Pacific.
■ CALIBRE: 150mm (5.9in); MAXIMUM RANGE: 20,117m (22,000yd); MAXIMUM RATE OF FIRE: 1–2rpm; AMMUNITION: Anti-personnel, high-explosive, shrapnel

Model No. 96 (1936) 150mm Howitzer

This was one of the finest field howitzers used by the Japanese Imperial Army during World War II. It was by far the most modern of all the field guns in service at the conclusion of the war.
■ CALIBRE: 150mm (5.9in); WEIGHT: 3975.7kg (8765lb) (in firing position); MAXIMUM RANGE: 20,117m (22,000yd); MAXIMUM RATE OF FIRE: 1–2rpm; AMMUNITION: High-explosive, anti-personnel, shrapnel, smoke, incendiary

ARMOURED CARS AND TANKS

During World War II, the Japanese Army employed both armoured cars and tanks as infantry-support weapons and for reconnaissance purposes. The following is a brief description of the most commonly used armoured cars and tanks employed by the Japanese during the conflict.

Armoured Cars
Model 25 'Vickers Crossley.'

This armoured car was used by the Japanese for reconnaissance and cavalry purposes. All of the machine guns found on this vehicle were Vickers. The guns were ball-mounted and had a limited traverse independent to that of the turret. The front wheels were single, while the rear wheels were dual drive. The chassis was a standard commercial type weighing 2844.9kg (2.8 tons).
■ WEIGHT: 5486.7kg (5.4 tons); LENGTH: 5.03m (16ft 6in); WIDTH: 1.88m (6ft 2in); GROUND CLEARANCE: 254mm (10in); CREW: Four; ARMOUR: 5.5mm (0.21in); ARMAMENT: Two Vickers machine guns; AMMUNITION: 3500 rounds; SPEED: 64km/h (40mph); RANGE OF ACTION: 200km (124 miles)

Model No. 92 (1932) 'Osaka'

The Model No. 92 (1932) 'Osaka' was a Japanese design built from a standard commercial chassis. The wheels were fitted with pneumatic tyres, the front single and the rear dual method. Machine guns were of the Vickers type; one was mounted in the front of the turret. The second machine gun was mounted in the front hull.

■ WEIGHT: 6502.7kg (6.4 tons); LENGTH: 5m (16ft 5in); WIDTH: 1.83m (6ft); HEIGHT: 2.64m (8ft 8in); CREW: Three to five; ARMOUR: 8–11mm (0.31–0.43in); ARMAMENT: Two machine guns; SPEED: 59.5km/h (37mph); RANGE: 241km (150 miles)

Model No. 93 (1933) 'Sumida'

The Model No. 93 (1933) 'Sumida' was designed specifically to operate on either roads or rails. The Japanese used this particular armoured car extensively in China. It came equipped with two types of wheels: flanged wheels which were used for operations on railroads; and rubber wheels which were used on highways and roads.

This vehicle would prove to be extremely useful for the Japanese forces fighting in the numerous counter-guerrilla campaigns which were conducted against the Nationalist forces in China.

Below: Japanese Model 25 Vickers Crossley armoured cars parade through the streets of Shanghai, China. They were armed only with a pair of Vickers machine guns in the rotating domed turret.

■ WEIGHT: 7620.4kg (7.5 tons); LENGTH: 6.55m (21ft 6in); WIDTH: 1.91m (6ft 3in); HEIGHT: 2.95m (9ft 8in); CREW: Six; ARMOUR: 10mm (0.39in); ARMAMENT: One machine gun in the turret; slits for rifles or machine guns; SPEED: 59.5km/h (37mph) (rail); 40.2km/h (25mph) (road); RANGE: 241km (150 miles)

Tanks

Mechanisation, particularly in the form of armour, came late to the Japanese Army. In fact, the Japanese Army did not produce tanks of its own until halfway through the interwar period, in 1929. By and large, the tanks found in Japanese service after that time came from certain British manufacturers (Vickers, Carden-Lloyd) as well as from the French (Renault). In fact, the Japanese entered World War II with scant tank forces; any tank capacity they did possess centred on tankettes (primarily amphibious) and light and medium tanks.

Tankette Model 94 (1932)

The Tankette Model 94 (1932) was used extensively in China as a cavalry and reconnaissance vehicle, as well as a towing and logistical carrier. The hull was of a riveted and welded construction.

■ WEIGHT: 3048.1kg (3 tons); LENGTH: 3.07m (10ft ½in); WIDTH: 1.60m (5ft 3in); HEIGHT: 1.63m (5ft 4in); CREW: Two; ARMOUR: 6–14mm (0.24–0.55in); SPEED: 40.2km/h (25mph); ARMAMENT: One 7.7mm (0.303in) ball-mounted machine gun; RANGE: 161km (100 miles)

Tankette Model No. 97 (1937)

The hull on the Model 97 Tankette was re-designed, as was the turret, to accommodate a 37mm (1.47in) gun, although a machine gun was sometimes used. As its powerplant, this tank was fitted with a four-cylinder diesel engine.

■ WEIGHT: 4572.2kg (4.5 tons); LENGTH: 3.66m (12ft); WIDTH: 1.83m (6ft); HEIGHT: 1.83m (6ft); CREW: Two; ARMOUR: 4–12mm (0.16–0.47in); SPEED: 45.1km/h (28mph); ARMAMENT: One 37mm gun; RANGE: 250km (155 miles)

Light Tank Model 93 (1933)

The Light Tank Model 93 (1933) was the earliest of light tanks to enter service with the Japanese armed forces during World War II.

■ WEIGHT: 7925.2kg (7.8 tons); LENGTH: 4.47m (14ft 8in); WIDTH: 1.80m (5ft 11in); HEIGHT: 1.83m (6ft); CREW: Three; ARMOUR: Up to 22mm (0.87in); SPEED: 45.1km/h (28mph); ARMAMENT: One light machine gun (hull); one light machine gun (turret); RANGE: 193km (120 miles)

Light Tank Model 93 (1933) (Improved)

The Light Tank Model 93 (1933) (Improved) was an improved version of the Model 93 light tank. In the new model, the suspension had four bogie wheels coupled in pairs via the traverse even lever.

Above: Japanese Type 94 tankettes move forward with their tracked trailers. This system was designed to provide a means of bringing ammunition up to the front lines safely. The tankette had a solitary machine gun in the turret for self-defence.

■ WEIGHT: 7925.2kg (7.8 tons); LENGTH: 4.47m (14ft 8in); WIDTH: 1.80m (5ft 11in); HEIGHT: 1.83m (6ft); CREW: Three; ARMOUR: Up to 22mm (0.87in); SPEED: 45.1km/h (28mph); ARMAMENT: One 37mm (1.47in) gun; one turret machine gun; RANGE: 193km (120 miles)

Light Tank Model 95 (1935)

The Light Tank Model 95 (1935) was the armoured vehicle most extensively used by Japanese forces during the course of World War II.

■ WEIGHT: 10,160.5kg (10 tons); LENGTH: 4.37m (14ft 4in); WIDTH: 2.06m (6ft 9in); HEIGHT: 2.28m (7ft 6in); CREW: Three; ARMOUR: 6–12mm (0.24–0.47in); SPEED: 45.1km/h (28mph); ARMAMENT: One 37mm (1.47in) gun; one 7.7mm (0.303in) machine gun (rear turret); one 7.7mm machine gun (hull); RANGE: 161km (100 miles)

Medium Tank Model 89 (1929)

The Medium Tank Model 89 (1929) was fitted with a medium anti-tank gun and a machine gun.

Above: Type 95 tanks move through paddy fields during an exercise conducted by the Japanese military Tank Training Institute near Tokyo on 22 September 1941. The Type 95 was armed only with a 37mm (1.45in) main gun.

■ WEIGHT: 13,208.6kg (13 tons); LENGTH: 5.87m (19ft 3in); WIDTH: 2.16m (7ft 1in); HEIGHT: 2.59m (8ft 6in); CREW: Four; ARMOUR: 6–17mm (0.24–0.67in); SPEED: 24.1km/h (15mph); ARMAMENT: One 57mm (2.24in) gun; one hull-mounted machine gun; one rear-turret machine gun; RANGE: 161km (100 miles)

Medium Tank Model No. 94 (1934)
■ WEIGHT: 15,240.7kg (15 tons); LENGTH: 7.01m (23ft); HEIGHT: 2.59m (8ft 6in); CREW: Four; ARMOUR: 6–17mm (0.24–0.67in); ARMAMENT: One 57mm (2.24in) gun; one hull-mounted and one rear-turret machine gun

Medium Tank Model 97 (1937)
The Japanese Medium Tank Model 97 (1937) was the most commonly used tank during World War II. Japanese infantrymen used this armoured vehicle extensively in Burma and China, as well as in the Central Pacific.
■ WEIGHT: 1031kg (15 tons); LENGTH: 5.49m (18ft); WIDTH: 2.34m (7ft 8in); HEIGHT: 2.34m (7ft 8in); CREW: Four; ARMOUR: 8–25mm (0.31–0.98in); SPEED: 40.3km/h (25mph); ARMAMENT: One

57mm (2.24in) gun; one hull-mounted and one rear-turret 7.7mm (0.303in) gun; RANGE: 161km (100 miles)

The Japanese likewise employed several amphibious tanks that weighed approximately 4064kg (4 tons), were armed with a 37mm (1.47in) gun and one machine gun, and were protected by up to 20mm (0.79in) of armour.

Not noted for their innovation in the field of armoured warfare, the Japanese introduced a new type of design for its amphibious tanks in late 1943. Most notable among this category was introduced in mid-1943; it had a simple one-piece hull construction and a turreted 37mm (1.47in) gun, and it was seen for the first time on Saipan in June 1944.

New Model Amphibious Tank
■ WEIGHT: 13,208.6kg (13 tons); LENGTH: 4.78m (15ft 8in); WIDTH: 2.79m (9ft 2in); HEIGHT: 2.29m (7ft 6in); CREW: Six; ARMOUR: Turret and sides: 13.2mm (0.52in); top: 6mm (0.24in); hull: 12mm (0.47in); ARMAMENT: One 37mm (1.47in) gun; one 7.7mm (0.303in) machine gun in hull-forward position and one 7.7mm (0.303in) coaxially mounted; RANGE: 200km (125 miles)

Below: A Type 3 Amphibious Tank sits abandoned along a road on the island of Saipan in 1944. The Japanese developed a number of amphibious tanks to aid their landing forces, but these were still outclassed by the latest Allied armour.

JAPANESE ARMY INSIGNIA

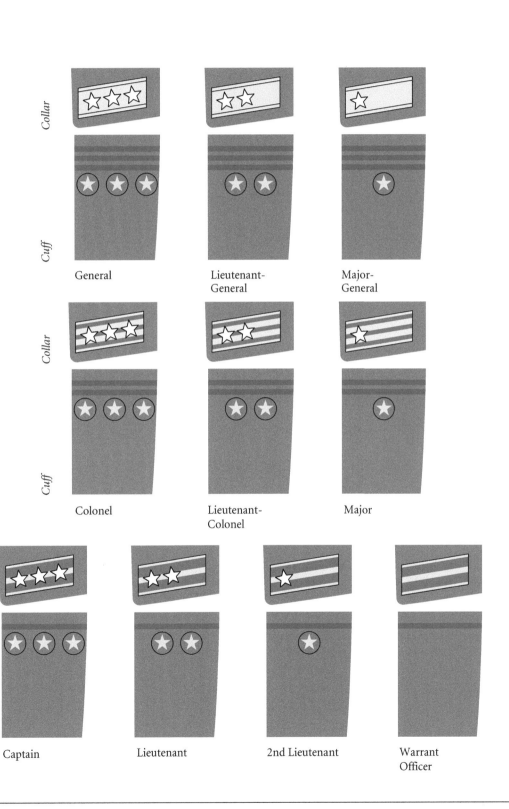

Collar

Cuff

General

Lieutenant-
General

Major-
General

Colonel

Lieutenant-
Colonel

Major

Captain

Lieutenant

2nd Lieutenant

Warrant
Officer

JAPANESE ARMY INSIGNIA

 Cap badge: Other Ranks

 *Cap badge:* Imperial Guards

 Cap badge: Officers

Collar

Sergeant Major

Sergeant

Corporal

Collar

Lance-Corporal

Superior Private

Private 1st Class

Collar

Private 2nd Class

Private

Officers

Sleeve

Warrant Officers

NCOs

Corporals

Sleeve

Corporal, acting
Sergeant

Private, acting
Corporal

Good Conduct
Stripe

INDEX

#0031 - 230118 - C0 - 285/213/6 - PB - 9781782746003